NO FEAR

SHAKESPEARE™

More
Reads

NO FEAR SHAKESPEARE

Antony and Cleopatra

As You Like It

The Comedy of Errors

Coriolanus

Hamlet

Henry IV, Parts One and Two

Henry V

Julius Caesar

King Lear

Macbeth

Measure for Measure

The Merchant of Venice

A Midsummer Night's Dream

Much Ado About Nothing

Othello

Richard III

Romeo and Juliet

Sonnets

The Taming of the Shrew

The Tempest

Twelfth Night

Two Gentlemen of Verona

Winter's Tale

NO FEAR
SHAKESPEARE™

A Midsummer Night's Dream

DELUXE STUDENT EDITION

There's matter in these sighs, these
profound heaves. You must translate.
'Tis fit we understand them.

(*Hamlet, IV.i.*)

Have you ever found yourself looking at a Shakespeare
play, then down at the footnotes, then back up at the play,
and still not understanding? You know what the individual
words mean, but they don't add up. SparkNotes' *No Fear
Shakespeare* will help you break through all that. Put the
pieces together with our easy-to-read translations. Soon
you'll be reading Shakespeare's own words fearlessly—
and actually enjoying it.

No Fear Shakespeare puts Shakespeare's language side-by-
side with a facing-page translation into modern English—
the kind of English people actually speak today. When
Shakespeare's words make your head spin, our translation
will help you sort out what's happening, who's saying
what, and why.

*spark notes

ISBN 978-1-4114-7969-2

Distributed in Canada by Sterling Publishing Co., Inc.
c/o Canadian Manda Group, 664 Annette Street
Toronto, Ontario M6S 2C8, Canada
Distributed in the United Kingdom by GMC Distribution Services
Castle Place, 166 High Street, Lewes, East Sussex BN7 1XU, England
Distributed in Australia by NewSouth Books
University of New South Wales, Sydney, NSW 2052, Australia

For information about custom editions, special sales, and premium
and corporate purchases, please contact Sterling Special Sales at
800-805-5489 or specialsales@sterlingpublishing.com.

Manufactured in Canada

Lot #:
2 4 6 8 10 9 7 5 3 1
05/20

sterlingpublishing.com
sparknotes.com

Cover design by Elizabeth Mihaltse Lindy
Interior design by Sharon Jacobs

CONTENTS

PART I

LITERATURE GUIDE

PART II

THE PLAY

PART III

STUDY GUIDE

NOTES

PART I

LITERATURE
GUIDE

NOTES

1

CONTEXT

THE MOST INFLUENTIAL WRITER in all of English literature, William Shakespeare was born in 1564 to a successful middle-class glove-maker in Stratford-upon-Avon, England. Shakespeare attended grammar school, but his formal education proceeded no farther. In 1582 he married an older woman, Anne Hathaway, and had three children with her. Around 1590 he left his family behind and traveled to London to work as an actor and playwright. Public and critical success quickly followed, and Shakespeare eventually became the most popular playwright in England and part-owner of the Globe Theater. His career bridged the reigns of Elizabeth I (ruled 1558–1603) and James I (ruled 1603–1625), and he was a favorite of both monarchs. Indeed, James granted Shakespeare's company the greatest possible compliment by bestowing upon its members the title of King's Men. Wealthy and renowned, Shakespeare retired to Stratford and died in 1616 at the age of fifty-two. At the time of Shakespeare's death, literary luminaries such as Ben Jonson hailed his works as timeless.

Shakespeare's works were collected and printed in various editions in the century following his death, and by the early eighteenth century his reputation as the greatest poet ever to write in English was well established. The unprecedented admiration garnered by his works led to a fierce curiosity about Shakespeare's life, but the dearth of biographical information has left many details of Shakespeare's personal history shrouded in mystery. Some people have concluded from this fact that Shakespeare's plays were really written by someone else—Francis Bacon and the Earl of Oxford are the two most popular candidates—but the support for this claim is overwhelmingly circumstantial, and the theory is not taken seriously by many scholars.

In the absence of credible evidence to the contrary, Shakespeare must be viewed as the author of the thirty-seven plays and 154 sonnets that bear his name. The legacy of this body of work is immense. A number of Shakespeare's plays seem to have transcended even the category of brilliance, becoming so influential as to profoundly affect the course of Western literature and culture ever after.

Written in the mid-1590s, probably shortly before Shakespeare turned to *Romeo and Juliet*, *A Midsummer Night's Dream* is one of his strangest and most delightful creations, and it marks a departure from his earlier works and from others of the English Renaissance. The play demonstrates both the extent of Shakespeare's learning and the expansiveness of his imagination. The range of references in the play is among its most extraordinary attributes: Shakespeare draws on sources as various as Greek mythology (Theseus, for instance, is loosely based on the Greek hero of the same name, and the play is peppered with references to Greek gods and goddesses); English country fairy lore (the character of Puck, or Robin Goodfellow, was a popular figure in sixteenth-century stories); and the theatrical practices of Shakespeare's London (the craftsmen's play refers to and parodies many conventions of English Renaissance theater, such as men playing the roles of women). Further, many of the characters are drawn from diverse texts: Titania comes from Ovid's *Metamorphoses*, and Oberon may have been taken from the medieval romance *Huan of Bordeaux*, translated by Lord Berners in the mid-1530s. Unlike the plots of many of Shakespeare's plays, however, the story in *A Midsummer Night's Dream* seems not to have been drawn from any particular source but rather to be the original product of the playwright's imagination.

NOTES

2

PLOT OVERVIEW

THESEUS, DUKE OF ATHENS, is preparing for his marriage to Hippolyta, queen of the Amazons, with a four-day festival of pomp and entertainment. He commissions his Master of the Revels, Philostrate, to find suitable amusements for the occasion. Egeus, an Athenian nobleman, marches into Theseus's court with his daughter, Hermia, and two young men, Demetrius and Lysander. Egeus wishes Hermia to marry Demetrius (who loves Hermia), but Hermia is in love with Lysander and refuses to comply. Egeus asks for the full penalty of law to fall on Hermia's head if she flouts her father's will. Theseus gives Hermia until his wedding to consider her options, warning her that disobeying her father's wishes could result in her being sent to a convent or even executed. Nonetheless, Hermia and Lysander plan to escape Athens the following night and marry in the house of Lysander's aunt, some seven leagues distant from the city. They make their intentions known to Hermia's friend Helena, who was once engaged to Demetrius and still loves him even though he jilted her after meeting Hermia. Hoping to regain his love, Helena tells Demetrius of the elopement that Hermia and Lysander have planned. At the appointed time, Demetrius stalks into the woods after his intended bride and her lover; Helena follows behind him.

In these same woods are two very different groups of characters. The first is a band of fairies, including Oberon, the fairy king, and Titania, his queen, who has recently returned from India to bless the marriage of Theseus and Hippolyta. The second is a band of Athenian craftsmen rehearsing a play that they hope to perform for the duke and his bride. Oberon and Titania are at odds over a young Indian prince given to Titania by the prince's mother; the boy is so beautiful that Oberon wishes to make him a knight, but Titania refuses. Seeking revenge, Oberon sends his merry servant, Puck, to acquire a magical flower, the juice of which can be spread over a sleeping person's eyelids to make that person fall in love with the first thing he or she sees upon waking. Puck obtains the flower, and Oberon tells him of his plan to spread its juice on the sleeping Titania's eyelids. Having seen Demetrius act cruelly toward Helena, he orders Puck to spread some of the juice on the eyelids of the young Athenian man. Puck encounters Lysander and Hermia; thinking that Lysander is the Athenian of whom Oberon spoke, Puck afflicts him with the love potion. Lysander happens to see Helena upon awaking and falls deeply in love with her, abandoning Hermia. As the night progresses and Puck attempts to undo his mistake, both Lysander and Demetrius end up in love with Helena, who believes that they are mocking her. Hermia becomes so jealous that she tries to challenge Helena to a fight. Demetrius and Lysander nearly do fight over Helena's love, but Puck confuses them by mimicking their voices, leading them apart until they are lost separately in the forest.

When Titania wakes, the first creature she sees is Bottom, the most ridiculous of the Athenian craftsmen, whose head Puck has mockingly transformed into that of an ass. Titania passes a ludicrous interlude doting on the ass-headed weaver. Eventually, Oberon obtains the Indian boy, Puck spreads the love potion on Lysander's eyelids, and by morning all is well. Theseus and Hippolyta discover the sleeping lovers in the forest and take them back to Athens to be married—Demetrius now loves Helena, and Lysander now loves Hermia. After the group wedding, the lovers watch Bottom and his fellow craftsmen perform their play, a fumbling, hilarious version of the story of Pyramus and Thisbe. When the play is completed, the lovers go to bed; the fairies briefly emerge to bless the sleeping couples with a protective charm and then disappear. Only Puck remains, to ask the audience for its forgiveness and approval and to urge it to remember the play as though it had all been a dream.

NOTES

CHAPTER

3

IN-DEPTH REVIEW OF CHARACTERS

PUCK

Also known as Robin Goodfellow, Puck is Oberon's jester, a mischievous fairy who delights in playing pranks on mortals. Though *A Midsummer Night's Dream* divides its action between several groups of characters, Puck is the closest thing the play has to a protagonist. His enchanting, mischievous spirit pervades the atmosphere, and his antics are responsible for many of the complications that propel the other main plots: he mistakes the young Athenians, applying the love potion to Lysander instead of Demetrius, thereby causing chaos within the group of young lovers; he also transforms Bottom's head into that of an ass.

OBERON

The king of the fairies, Oberon is initially at odds with his wife, Titania, because she refuses to relinquish control of a young Indian prince whom he wants for a knight. Oberon's desire for revenge on Titania leads him to send Puck to obtain the love-potion flower that creates so much of the play's confusion and farce.

TITANIA

The beautiful queen of the fairies, Titania resists the attempts of her husband, Oberon, to make a knight of the young Indian prince that she has been given. Titania's brief, potion-induced love for Nick Bottom, whose head Puck has transformed into that of an ass, yields the play's foremost example of the contrast motif.

LYSANDER

A young man of Athens, in love with Hermia. Lysander's relationship with Hermia invokes the theme of love's difficulty: he cannot marry her openly because Egeus, her father, wishes her to wed Demetrius; when Lysander and Hermia run away into the forest, Lysander becomes the victim of misapplied magic and wakes up in love with Helena.

DEMETRIUS

A young man of Athens, initially in love with Hermia and ultimately in love with Helena. Demetrius's obstinate pursuit of Hermia throws love out of balance among the quartet of Athenian youths and precludes a symmetrical two-couple arrangement.

HERMIA

Egeus's daughter, a young woman of Athens. Hermia is in love with Lysander and is a childhood friend of Helena. As a result of the fairies' mischief with Oberon's love potion, both Lysander and Demetrius suddenly fall in love with Helena. Self-conscious about her short stature, Hermia suspects that Helena has wooed the men with her height. By morning, however, Puck has sorted matters out with the love potion, and Lysander's love for Hermia is restored.

HELENA

A young woman of Athens in love with Demetrius. Demetrius and Helena were once betrothed, but when Demetrius met Helena's friend Hermia, he fell in love with her and abandoned Helena. Lacking confidence in her looks, Helena thinks that Demetrius and Lysander are mocking her when the fairies' mischief causes them to fall in love with her.

EGEUS

Hermia's father, who brings a complaint against his daughter to Theseus: Egeus has given Demetrius permission to marry Hermia, but Hermia, in love with Lysander, refuses to marry Demetrius. Egeus's severe insistence that Hermia either respect his wishes or be held accountable to Athenian law places him squarely outside the whimsical dream realm of the forest.

THESEUS

The heroic duke of Athens, engaged to Hippolyta. Theseus represents power and order throughout the play. He appears only at the beginning and end of the story, removed from the dreamlike events of the forest.

HIPPOLYTA

The legendary queen of the Amazons, engaged to Theseus. Like Theseus, she symbolizes order.

NICK BOTTOM

The overconfident weaver chosen to play Pyramus in the craftsmen's play for Theseus's marriage celebration. Bottom is full of advice and self-confidence but frequently makes silly mistakes and misuses language. His simultaneous nonchalance about the beautiful Titania's sudden love for him and unawareness of the fact that Puck has transformed his head into that of an ass mark the pinnacle of his foolish arrogance.

PETER QUINCE

A carpenter and the nominal leader of the craftsmen's attempt to put on a play for Theseus's marriage celebration. Quince is often shoved aside by the abundantly confident Bottom. During the craftsmen's play, Quince plays the Prologue.

LITERATURE GUIDE

FRANCIS FLUTE

The bellows-mender chosen to play Thisbe in the craftsmen's play for Theseus's marriage celebration. Forced to play a young girl in love, the bearded craftsman determines to speak his lines in a high, squeaky voice.

ROBIN STARVELING

The tailor chosen to play Thisbe's mother in the craftsmen's play for Theseus's marriage celebration. He ends up playing the part of Moonshine.

TOM SNOUT

The tinker chosen to play Pyramus's father in the craftsmen's play for Theseus's marriage celebration. He ends up playing the part of Wall, dividing the two lovers.

SNUG

The joiner chosen to play the lion in the craftsmen's play for Theseus's marriage celebration. Snug worries that his roaring will frighten the ladies in the audience.

PHILOSTRATE

Theseus's Master of the Revels, responsible for organizing the entertainment for the duke's marriage celebration.

NOTES

NOTES

CHAPTER

4

ANALYSIS OF MAJOR CHARACTERS

PUCK

Though there is little character development in *A Midsummer Night's Dream* and no true protagonist, critics generally point to Puck as the most important character in the play. The mischievous, quick-witted sprite sets many of the play's events in motion with his magic, by means of both deliberate pranks on the human characters (transforming Bottom's head into that of an ass) and unfortunate mistakes (smearing the love potion on Lysander's eyelids instead of Demetrius's).

More important, Puck's capricious spirit, magical fancy, fun-loving humor, and lovely, evocative language permeate the atmosphere of the play. Wild contrasts, such as the implicit comparison between the rough, earthy craftsmen and the delicate, graceful fairies, dominate *A Midsummer Night's Dream*. Puck seems to illustrate many of these contrasts within his own character: he is graceful but not so saccharine as the other fairies; as Oberon's jester, he is given to a certain coarseness, which leads him to transform Bottom's head into that of an ass merely for the sake of enjoyment. He is goodhearted but capable of cruel tricks. Finally, whereas most of the fairies are beautiful and ethereal, Puck is often portrayed as somewhat bizarre looking. Indeed, another fairy mentions that some call Puck a "hobgoblin," a term whose connotations are decidedly less glamorous than those of "fairy" (II.i.).

NICK BOTTOM

Whereas Puck's humor is often mischievous and subtle, the comedy surrounding the overconfident weaver Nick Bottom is hilariously overt. The central figure in the subplot involving the craftsmen's production of the Pyramus and Thisbe story, Bottom dominates his fellow actors with an extraordinary belief in his own abilities (he thinks he is perfect for every part in the play) and his comical incompetence (he is a terrible actor and frequently makes rhetorical and grammatical mistakes in his speech). The humor surrounding Bottom often stems from the fact that he is totally unaware of his own ridiculousness; his speeches are overdramatic and self-aggrandizing, and he seems to believe that everyone takes him as seriously as he does himself. This foolish self-importance reaches its pinnacle after Puck transforms Bottom's head into that of an ass. When Titania, whose eyes have been anointed with a love potion, falls in love with the now ass-headed Bottom, he believes that the devotion of the beautiful, magical fairy queen is nothing out of the ordinary and that all of the trappings of her affection, including having servants attend him, are his proper due. His unawareness of the fact that his head has been transformed into that of an ass parallels his inability to perceive the absurdity of the idea that Titania could fall in love with him.

HELENA

Although Puck and Bottom stand out as the most personable characters in *A Midsummer Night's Dream*, they themselves are not involved in the main dramatic events. Of the other characters, Helena, the lovesick young woman desperately in love with Demetrius, is perhaps the most fully drawn. Among the quartet of Athenian lovers, Helena is the one who thinks most about the nature of love—which makes sense, given that at the beginning of the play she is left out of the love triangle involving Lysander, Hermia, and Demetrius. She says, "Love looks not with the eyes, but with the mind," believing that Demetrius has built up a fantastic notion of Hermia's beauty that prevents him from recognizing Helena's own beauty (I.i.). Utterly faithful to Demetrius despite her recognition of his shortcomings, Helena sets out to win his love by telling him about the plan of Lysander and Hermia to elope into the forest. Once Helena enters the forest, many of her traits are drawn out by the confusion that the love potion engenders: compared to the other lovers, she is extremely unsure of herself, worrying about her appearance and believing that Lysander is mocking her when he declares his love for her.

NOTES

NOTES

PART II

THE PLAY

NO FEAR SHAKESPEARE™

NOTES

5

A Midsummer Night's Dream

THE ORIGINAL PLAY
WITH A MODERN TRANSLATION

William Shakespeare

NO FEAR SHAKESPEARE

CHARACTER LIST*

Theseus

Hippolyta

Egeus

Hermia

Lysander

Demetrius

Helena

Robin Goodfellow

Oberon

Titania

Nick Bottom

Peter Quince

Francis Flute

Robin Starveling

Tom Snout

Snug

Philostrate

Peaseblossom, Cobweb, Mote,
and Mustardseed

*See page 11 for an in-depth review of the characters.

ACT ONE

ACT TWO

ACT THREE

ACT FOUR

ACT FIVE

ACT ONE

Scene 1

Enter THESEUS, HIPPOLYTA, *and* PHILOSTRATE, *with others*

THESEUS

Now, fair Hippolyta, our nuptial hour
Draws on apace. Four happy days bring in
Another moon. But oh, methinks how slow
This old moon wanes! She lingers my desires,

5 Like to a stepdame or a dowager
Long withering out a young man's revenue.

HIPPOLYTA

Four days will quickly steep themselves in night.
Four nights will quickly dream away the time.
And then the moon, like to a silver bow

10 New bent in heaven, shall behold the night
Of our solemnities.

THESEUS

                      Go, Philostrate,
Stir up the Athenian youth to merriments.
Awake the pert and nimble spirit of mirth.
Turn melancholy forth to funerals.

15 The pale companion is not for our pomp.

Exit PHILOSTRATE

Hippolyta, I wooed thee with my sword
And won thy love doing thee injuries.
But I will wed thee in another key,
With pomp, with triumph, and with reveling.

Enter EGEUS *and his daughter* HERMIA, *and* LYSANDER *and*
DEMETRIUS

EGEUS

20 Happy be Theseus, our renownèd duke.

ACT ONE

Scene 1

THESEUS and HIPPOLYTA enter with PHILOSTRATE and others.

THESEUS

Our wedding day is almost here, my beautiful Hippolyta. We'll be getting married in four days, on the day of the new moon. But it seems to me that the days are passing too slowly—the old moon is taking too long to fade away! That old, slow moon is keeping me from getting what I want, just like an old widow makes her stepson wait to get his inheritance.

HIPPOLYTA

No, you'll see, four days will quickly turn into four nights. And since we dream at night, time passes quickly then. Finally the new moon, curved like a silver bow in the sky, will look down on our wedding celebration.

THESEUS

Go, Philostrate, get the young people of Athens ready to celebrate and have a good time. Sadness is only appropriate for funerals. We don't want it at our festivities.

PHILOSTRATE exits.

Hippolyta, I wooed you with violence, using my sword, and got you to fall in love with me by injuring you. But I'll marry you under different circumstances—with extravagant festivals, public festivities, and celebration.

EGEUS enters with his daughter HERMIA, and LYSANDER and DEMETRIUS.

EGEUS

Long live Theseus, our famous and respected duke!

THESEUS
Thanks, good Egeus. What's the news with thee?

EGEUS
Full of vexation come I with complaint
Against my child, my daughter Hermia.—
Stand forth, Demetrius.—My noble lord,
25   This man hath my consent to marry her.—
Stand forth, Lysander.—And my gracious duke,
This man hath bewitched the bosom of my child.—
Thou, thou, Lysander, thou hast given her rhymes,
And interchanged love tokens with my child.
30   Thou hast by moonlight at her window sung
With feigning voice verses of feigning love,
And stol'n the impression of her fantasy
With bracelets of thy hair, rings, gauds, conceits,
Knacks, trifles, nosegays, sweetmeats—messengers
35   Of strong prevailment in unhardened youth.
With cunning hast thou filched my daughter's heart,
Turned her obedience (which is due to me)
To stubborn harshness.—And, my gracious duke,
Be it so she will not here before your grace
40   Consent to marry with Demetrius,
I beg the ancient privilege of Athens.
As she is mine, I may dispose of her—
Which shall be either to this gentleman
Or to her death—according to our law
45   Immediately provided in that case.

THESEUS
What say you, Hermia? Be advised, fair maid:
To you your father should be as a god,
One that composed your beauties, yea, and one
To whom you are but as a form in wax,
50   By him imprinted and within his power
To leave the figure or disfigure it.
Demetrius is a worthy gentleman.

ACT ONE

THESEUS

Thanks, good Egeus. What's new with you?

EGEUS

I'm here, full of anger, to complain about my daughter Hermia.—Step forward, Demetrius.—My lord, this man, Demetrius, has my permission to marry her.—Step forward, Lysander.—But this other man, Lysander, has cast a magic spell over my child's heart.—You, you, Lysander, you've given her poems, and exchanged tokens of love with my daughter. You've pretended to be in love with her, singing fake love songs softly at her window by moonlight, and you've captured her imagination by giving her locks of your hair, rings, toys, trinkets, knickknacks, little presents, flowers, and candies—things that can really influence an impressionable young person. You've connived to steal my daughter's heart, making her stubborn and harsh instead of obedient (like she should be).—And, my gracious duke, if she won't agree to marry Demetrius right now, I ask you to let me exercise the right that all fathers have in Athens. Since she belongs to me, I can do what I want with her—as the law says: I can either make her marry Demetrius—or have her killed.

THESEUS

What do you have to say for yourself, Hermia? Think carefully, pretty girl. You should think of your father as a god, since he's the one who gave you your beauty. To him, you're like a figure that he's sculpted out of wax, and he has the power to keep that figure intact or to disfigure it. Demetrius is an admirable man.

HERMIA
So is Lysander.

THESEUS
In himself he is.
But in this kind, wanting your father's voice,
55   The other must be held the worthier.

HERMIA
I would my father looked but with my eyes.

THESEUS
Rather your eyes must with his judgment look.

HERMIA
I do entreat your grace to pardon me.
I know not by what power I am made bold
60   Nor how it may concern my modesty
In such a presence here to plead my thoughts,
But I beseech your grace that I may know
The worst that may befall me in this case,
If I refuse to wed Demetrius.

THESEUS
65   Either to die the death or to abjure
Forever the society of men.
Therefore, fair Hermia, question your desires.
Know of your youth. Examine well your blood—
Whether, if you yield not to your father's choice,
70   You can endure the livery of a nun,
For aye to be in shady cloister mewed,
To live a barren sister all your life,
Chanting faint hymns to the cold, fruitless moon.
Thrice-blessèd they that master so their blood
75   To undergo such maiden pilgrimage.
But earthlier happy is the rose distilled
Than that which, withering on the virgin thorn,
Grows, lives, and dies in single blessedness.

HERMIA

So is Lysander.

THESEUS

You're right, Lysander's admirable too. But since your father doesn't want him to marry you, you have to consider Demetrius to be the better man.

HERMIA

I wish my father could see them with my eyes.

THESEUS

No, you must see them as your father sees them.

HERMIA

Your grace, please forgive me. I don't know what makes me think I can say this, and I don't know if speaking my mind to such a powerful and noble person as yourself will damage my reputation for modesty. But please, tell me the worst thing that could happen to me if I refuse to marry Demetrius.

THESEUS

You'll either be executed or you'll never see another man again. So think carefully about what you want, beautiful Hermia. Consider how young you are, and question your feelings. Then decide whether you could stand to be a nun, wearing a priestess's habit and caged up in a cloister forever, living your entire life without a husband or children, weakly chanting hymns to the cold and virginal goddess of the moon. People who can restrain their passions and stay virgins forever are holy. But although a virgin priestess might be rewarded in heaven, a married woman is happier on Earth. A married woman is like a rose who is picked and made into a beautiful perfume, while a priestess just withers away on the stem.

HERMIA

So will I grow, so live, so die, my lord,
80   Ere I will my virgin patent up
Unto his lordship, whose unwishèd yoke
My soul consents not to give sovereignty.

THESEUS

Take time to pause, and by the next new moon—
The sealing day betwixt my love and me
85   For everlasting bond of fellowship—
Upon that day either prepare to die
For disobedience to your father's will,
Or else to wed Demetrius, as he would,
Or on Diana's altar to protest
90   For aye austerity and single life.

DEMETRIUS

Relent, sweet Hermia—And, Lysander, yield
Thy crazèd title to my certain right.

LYSANDER

You have her father's love, Demetrius.
Let me have Hermia's. Do you marry him.

EGEUS

95   Scornful Lysander, true, he hath my love,
And what is mine my love shall render him.
And she is mine, and all my right of her
I do estate unto Demetrius.

LYSANDER

(to THESEUS*)* I am, my lord, as well derived as he,
100   As well possessed. My love is more than his.
My fortunes every way as fairly ranked,
(If not with vantage) as Demetrius'.
And—which is more than all these boasts can be—
I am beloved of beauteous Hermia.
105   Why should not I then prosecute my right?
Demetrius, I'll avouch it to his head,
Made love to Nedar's daughter, Helena,
And won her soul. And she, sweet lady, dotes,

HERMIA

I'd rather wither away than give up my virginity to someone I don't love.

THESEUS

Take some time to think about this. By the time of the next new moon—the day when Hippolyta and I will be married—be ready either to be executed for disobeying your father, to marry Demetrius as your father wishes, or to take a vow to spend the rest of your life as a virgin priestess of the moon goddess.

DEMETRIUS

Please give in, sweet Hermia.—And Lysander, stop acting like she's yours. I've got more of a right to her than you do.

LYSANDER

Her father loves you, Demetrius. So why don't you marry him and let me have Hermia?

EGEUS

It's true, rude Lysander, I do love him. That's why I'm giving him my daughter. She's mine, and I'm giving her to Demetrius.

LYSANDER

(to THESEUS*)* My lord, I'm just as noble and rich as he is. I love Hermia more than he does. My prospects are as good as his, if not better. And beautiful Hermia loves me—which is more important than all those other things I'm bragging about. Why shouldn't I be able to marry her? Demetrius—and I'll say this to his face—courted Nedar's daughter, Helena, and made her fall in love with him. That sweet lady, Helena, loves devoutly. She adores this horrible and unfaithful man.

ACT ONE

Devoutly dotes, dotes in idolatry
110   Upon this spotted and inconstant man.

THESEUS
I must confess that I have heard so much
And with Demetrius thought to have spoke thereof,
But being overfull of self-affairs,
My mind did lose it.—But, Demetrius, come.
115   And come, Egeus. You shall go with me.
I have some private schooling for you both.—
For you, fair Hermia, look you arm yourself
To fit your fancies to your father's will,
Or else the law of Athens yields you up
120   (Which by no means we may extenuate)
To death, or to a vow of single life.—
Come, my Hippolyta. What cheer, my love?—
Demetrius and Egeus, go along.
I must employ you in some business
125   Against our nuptial and confer with you
Of something nearly that concerns yourselves.

EGEUS
With duty and desire we follow you.

Exeunt. Manent LYSANDER *and* HERMIA

LYSANDER
How now, my love? Why is your cheek so pale?
How chance the roses there do fade so fast?

HERMIA
130   Belike for want of rain, which I could well
Beteem them from the tempest of my eyes.

LYSANDER
Ay me! For aught that I could ever read,
Could ever hear by tale or history,
The course of true love never did run smooth.
135   But either it was different in blood—

THESEUS

I have to admit I've heard something about that, and meant to ask Demetrius about it, but I was too busy with personal matters and it slipped my mind.—Anyway, Demetrius and Egeus, both of you, come with me. I want to say a few things to you in private.—As for you, beautiful Hermia, get ready to do what your father wants, because otherwise the law says that you must die or become a nun, and there's nothing I can do about that.—Come with me, Hippolyta. How are you, my love?—Demetrius and Egeus, come with us. I want you to do some things for our wedding, and I also want to discuss something that concerns you both.

EGEUS

We're following you not only because it is our duty, but also because we want to.

They all exit except LYSANDER *and* HERMIA.

LYSANDER

What's going on, my love? Why are you so pale? Why have your rosy cheeks faded so quickly?

HERMIA

Probably because my cheeks' roses needed rain, which I could easily give them with all the tears in my eyes.

LYSANDER

Oh, honey! Listen, in books they say that true love always faces obstacles. Either the lovers have different social standings—

HERMIA
    O cross! Too high to be enthralled to low.

LYSANDER
    Or else misgraffèd in respect of years—

HERMIA
    O spite! Too old to be engaged to young.

LYSANDER
    Or else it stood upon the choice of friends—

HERMIA
140   O hell, to choose love by another's eyes!

LYSANDER
    Or, if there were a sympathy in choice,
    War, death, or sickness did lay siege to it,
    Making it momentary as a sound,
    Swift as a shadow, short as any dream,
145   Brief as the lightning in the collied night;
    That, in a spleen, unfolds both heaven and Earth,
    And ere a man hath power to say "Behold!"
    The jaws of darkness do devour it up.
    So quick bright things come to confusion.

HERMIA
150   If then true lovers have been ever crossed,
    It stands as an edict in destiny.
    Then let us teach our trial patience,
    Because it is a customary cross,
    As due to love as thoughts and dreams and sighs,
155   Wishes and tears, poor fancy's followers.

LYSANDER
    A good persuasion. Therefore, hear me, Hermia.
    I have a widow aunt, a dowager
    Of great revenue, and she hath no child.
    From Athens is her house remote seven leagues,
160   And she respects me as her only son.
    There, gentle Hermia, may I marry thee.
    And to that place the sharp Athenian law
    Cannot pursue us. If thou lovest me then,

HERMIA

Oh, what an obstacle that would be! Imagine being too high on the social ladder, and falling in love with someone beneath you.

LYSANDER

Or else they were very different ages—

HERMIA

How awful! Being too old to marry someone young.

LYSANDER

Or else their guardians and advisors said no—

HERMIA

What hell, to have your love life determined by someone else!

LYSANDER

Or, even if the lovers are a good match, their love might be ruined by war, death, or sickness, so that the affair only lasts an instant. Their time together might be as fleeting as a shadow or as short as a dream, lasting only as long as it takes a lightning bolt to flash across the sky. Before you can say "look," it's gone. That's how intense things like love are quickly destroyed.

HERMIA

If true lovers are always thwarted, then it must be a rule of fate. So let's try to be patient as we deal with our problem. It's as normal a part of love as dreams, sighs, wishes, and tears.

LYSANDER

That's the right attitude. So, listen, Hermia. I have an aunt who is a widow, who's very rich and doesn't have any children. She lives about twenty miles from Athens, and she thinks of me as a son. I could marry you there, gentle Hermia, where the strict laws of Athens can't touch us. So here's the plan. If you love me, sneak

Steal forth thy father's house tomorrow night.
165 And in the wood, a league without the town—
Where I did meet thee once with Helena
To do observance to a morn of May—
There will I stay for thee.

HERMIA
My good Lysander!
I swear to thee by Cupid's strongest bow,
170 By his best arrow with the golden head,
By the simplicity of Venus' doves,
By that which knitteth souls and prospers loves,
And by that fire which burned the Carthage queen
When the false Troyan under sail was seen,
175 By all the vows that ever men have broke
(In number more than ever women spoke),
In that same place thou hast appointed me,
Tomorrow truly will I meet with thee.

LYSANDER
Keep promise, love. Look, here comes Helena.

Enter HELENA

HERMIA
180 Godspeed, fair Helena! Whither away?

HELENA
Call you me "fair"? That "fair" again unsay.
Demetrius loves your fair. O happy fair!
Your eyes are lodestars, and your tongue's sweet air
More tunable than lark to shepherd's ear
185 When wheat is green, when hawthorn buds appear.
Sickness is catching. Oh, were favor so,
Yours would I catch, fair Hermia, ere I go.
My ear should catch your voice. My eye, your eye.
My tongue should catch your tongue's sweet melody.
190 Were the world mine, Demetrius being bated,
The rest I'd give to be to you translated.

out of your father's house tomorrow night and meet me in the forest a few miles outside of town. You remember the place—I met you there once with Helena to celebrate May Day.—I'll wait for you there.

HERMIA

Oh, Lysander, I swear I'll be there tomorrow. I swear by Cupid's strongest bow and his best gold-tipped arrow, by the Goddess of Love's innocent doves, by everything that ties lovers together, by the bonfire where Queen Dido burned herself to death when her lover Aeneas jilted her, and by all the promises that men have broken (and men have broken more promises than women have ever made). I give you my word, I will meet you at that spot tomorrow.

LYSANDER

Keep your promise, my love. Look, here comes Helena.

HELENA *enters.*

HERMIA

Hello, beautiful Helena! Where are you going?

HELENA

Did you just call me "beautiful"? Take it back. You're the beautiful one as far as Demetrius is concerned. Oh, you're so lucky! Your eyes are like stars, and your voice is more musical than a lark's song is to a shepherd in the springtime. Sickness is contagious—I wish beauty were contagious too! I would catch your good looks before I left. My ear would be infected by your voice, my eye by your eye, and my tongue would come down with a bad case of your melodious speech. If the world were mine, I'd give it all up—everything except Demetrius—to be you. Oh, teach me how you look

O, teach me how you look and with what art
You sway the motion of Demetrius' heart.

HERMIA
I frown upon him, yet he loves me still.

HELENA
195   Oh, that your frowns would teach my smiles such skill!

HERMIA
I give him curses, yet he gives me love.

HELENA
Oh, that my prayers could such affection move!

HERMIA
The more I hate, the more he follows me.

HELENA
The more I love, the more he hateth me.

HERMIA
200   His folly, Helena, is no fault of mine.

HELENA
None, but your beauty. Would that fault were mine!

HERMIA
Take comfort. He no more shall see my face.
Lysander and myself will fly this place.
Before the time I did Lysander see
205   Seemed Athens as a paradise to me.
Oh, then, what graces in my love do dwell,
That he hath turned a heaven unto a hell!

LYSANDER
Helen, to you our minds we will unfold.
Tomorrow night when Phoebe doth behold
210   Her silver visage in the watery glass,
Decking with liquid pearl the bladed grass
(A time that lovers' flights doth still conceal),
Through Athens' gates have we devised to steal.

HERMIA
(to HELENA) And in the wood where often you and I
215   Upon faint primrose beds were wont to lie,
Emptying our bosoms of their counsel sweet,

the way you do, and which tricks you used to make Demetrius fall in love with you.

HERMIA

I frown at him, but he still loves me.

HELENA

Oh, if only my smiles could inspire love as effectively as your frowns!

HERMIA

I curse him, but he loves me.

HELENA

If only my prayers could inspire that kind of affection!

HERMIA

The more I hate him, the more he follows me around.

HELENA

The more I love him, the more he hates me.

HERMIA

It's not my fault he acts like that, Helena.

HELENA

That's true, it's your beauty's fault. I wish I had a fault like that!

HERMIA

Don't worry. He won't see my face ever again. Lysander and I are running away from here. Before I saw Lysander, Athens seemed like paradise to me. But Lysander's so attractive that he's turned heaven into hell!

LYSANDER

Helena, we'll tell you about our secret plan. Tomorrow night, when the moon shines on the water and decorates the grass with tiny beads of pearly light (the time of night that always hides runaway lovers), we plan to sneak out of Athens.

HERMIA

(to HELENA*)* In the woods where you and I used to lounge around on the pale primroses, telling each other sweet secrets—that's where Lysander and I will

There my Lysander and myself shall meet.
And thence from Athens turn away our eyes
To seek new friends and stranger companies.
220 Farewell, sweet playfellow. Pray thou for us.
And good luck grant thee thy Demetrius!—
Keep word, Lysander. We must starve our sight
From lovers' food till morrow deep midnight.

LYSANDER
I will, my Hermia.

Exit HERMIA

Helena, adieu.
225 As you on him, Demetrius dote on you!

Exit LYSANDER

HELENA
How happy some o'er other some can be!
Through Athens I am thought as fair as she.
But what of that? Demetrius thinks not so.
He will not know what all but he do know.
230 And as he errs, doting on Hermia's eyes,
So I, admiring of his qualities.
Things base and vile, holding no quantity,
Love can transpose to form and dignity.
Love looks not with the eyes but with the mind.
235 And therefore is winged Cupid painted blind.
Nor hath Love's mind of any judgment taste—
Wings and no eyes figure unheedy haste.
And therefore is Love said to be a child,
Because in choice he is so oft beguiled.
240 As waggish boys in game themselves forswear,
So the boy Love is perjured everywhere.
For ere Demetrius looked on Hermia's eyne,
He hailed down oaths that he was only mine.
And when this hail some heat from Hermia felt,

meet. From then on we'll turn our backs on Athens. We'll look for new friends and keep the company of strangers. Goodbye, old friend. Pray for us, and I hope you win over Demetrius!—Keep your promise, Lysander. We need to stay away from each other until midnight tomorrow.

LYSANDER

I will, my Hermia.

HERMIA *exits*.

Goodbye, Helena. I hope Demetrius comes to love you as much as you love him!

LYSANDER *exits*.

HELENA

It's amazing how much happier some people are than others! People throughout Athens think I'm as beautiful as Hermia. But so what? Demetrius doesn't think so, and that's all that matters. He refuses to admit what everyone else knows. But even though he's making a mistake by obsessing over Hermia so much, I'm also making a mistake, since I obsess over him. Love can make worthless things beautiful. When we're in love, we don't see with our eyes but with our minds. That's why paintings of Cupid, the god of love, always show him as blind. And love doesn't have good judgment either—Cupid, has wings and no eyes, so he's bound to be reckless and hasty. That's why they say love is a child. because it makes such bad choices. Just as boys like to play games by telling lies, Cupid breaks his promises all the time. Before Demetrius ever saw Hermia, he showered me with promises and swore he'd be mine forever. But when he got all hot and

245   So he dissolved, and showers of oaths did melt.
I will go tell him of fair Hermia's flight.
Then to the wood will he tomorrow night
Pursue her. And for this intelligence
If I have thanks, it is a dear expense.
250   But herein mean I to enrich my pain,
To have his sight thither and back again.

Exit

bothered over Hermia, his promises melted away. I'll go tell Demetrius that Hermia is running away tomorrow night. He'll run after her. If he's grateful to me for this information, it'll be worth my pain in helping him pursue my rival Hermia. At least I'll get to see him when he goes, and then again when he comes back.

HERMIA *exits.*

ACT ONE, Scene 2

Enter QUINCE *the carpenter, and* SNUG *the joiner, and*
BOTTOM *the weaver, and* FLUTE *the bellows-mender, and*
SNOUT *the tinker, and* STARVELING *the tailor*

QUINCE
Is all our company here?

BOTTOM
You were best to call them generally, man by man,
according to the scrip.

QUINCE
Here is the scroll of every man's name which is thought fit,
5   through all Athens, to play in our interlude before the duke
and the duchess, on his wedding day at night.

BOTTOM
First, good Peter Quince, say what the play treats on, then
read the names of the actors, and so grow to a point.

QUINCE
Marry, our play is The most lamentable comedy and most
10   *cruel death of Pyramus and Thisbe.*

BOTTOM
A very good piece of work, I assure you, and a merry.—
Now, good Peter Quince, call forth your actors by the
scroll.—Masters, spread yourselves.

QUINCE
Answer as I call you.—Nick Bottom, the weaver?

BOTTOM
15   Ready. Name what part I am for and proceed.

QUINCE
You, Nick Bottom, are set down for Pyramus.

ACT ONE, Scene 2

QUINCE, the carpenter, enters with SNUG, the cabinetmaker;
BOTTOM, the weaver; FLUTE, the bellows-repairman;
SNOUT, the handyman; and STARVELING, the tailor.

QUINCE

Is everyone here?

BOTTOM

Bottom means "individually," not "generally." Bottom frequently makes mistakes with words.

You should call their names generally, one person at a time, in the order in which their names appear on this piece of paper.

QUINCE

This is a list of the names of all the men in Athens who are good enough to act in the play we're going to perform for the duke and duchess on their wedding night.

BOTTOM

First, Peter Quince, tell us what the play is about, then read the names of the actors, and then shut up.

QUINCE

All right. Our play is called *A Very Tragic Comedy About the Horrible Deaths of Pyramus and Thisbe.*

BOTTOM

Let me tell you, it's a great piece of work, and very—funny.—Now, Peter Quince, call the names of the actors on the list. Men, gather around him.

QUINCE

Answer when I call your name.—Nick Bottom, the weaver?

BOTTOM

Here. Tell me which part I'm going to play, then go on.

QUINCE

You, Nick Bottom, have been cast as Pyramus.

BOTTOM

What is Pyramus? A lover or a tyrant?

QUINCE

A lover that kills himself, most gallant, for love.

BOTTOM

That will ask some tears in the true performing of it. If I do
20   it, let the audience look to their eyes. I will move storms. I
will condole in some measure.—To the rest.—Yet my chief
humor is for a tyrant. I could play Ercles rarely, or a part to
tear a cat in to make all split.

> *The raging rocks*
25   *And shivering shocks*
> *Shall break the locks*
> *Of prison gates.*
> *And Phoebus' car*
> *Shall shine from far*
30   *And make and mar*
> *The foolish Fates.*

This was lofty!—Now name the rest of the players.—This
is Ercles' vein, a tyrant's vein. A lover is more condoling.

QUINCE

Francis Flute, the bellows-mender?

FLUTE

35   Here, Peter Quince.

QUINCE

Flute, you must take Thisbe on you.

BOTTOM

Medieval and Renaissance plays often featured tyrant characters— kings who gave long, ranting speeches.

What's Pyramus? A lover or a tyrant?

QUINCE

A lover who kills himself very nobly for love.

BOTTOM

I'll have to cry to make my performance believable. And as soon as I start crying, oh boy, the audience had better watch out, because they'll start crying too. I'll make tears pour out of their eyes like rainstorms. I'll moan very believably.—Name the other actors.—But I'm really in the mood to play a tyrant. I could do a great job with Hercules, or any other part that requires ranting and raving. I would rant and rave really well. Like this, listen.

> *The raging rocks*
> *And shivering shocks*
> *Will break the locks*
> *Of prison gates.*
> *And the sun-god's car*
> *Will shine from far*
> *Away, and make and mar*
> *Foolish fate.*

Oh, that was truly inspired!—Now tell us who the other actors are.—By the way, my performance just now was in the style of Hercules, the tyrant style. A lover would have to be weepier, of course.

QUINCE

Francis Flute, the bellows-repairman?

FLUTE

Here, Peter Quince.

QUINCE

Flute, you'll be playing the role of Thisbe.

ACT ONE

FLUTE
What is Thisbe? A wandering knight?

QUINCE
It is the lady that Pyramus must love.

FLUTE
Nay, faith, let me not play a woman. I have a beard coming.

QUINCE
40   That's all one. You shall play it in a mask, and you may
speak as small as you will.

BOTTOM
An I may hide my face, let me play Thisbe too! I'll speak in
a monstrous little voice: "Thisne, Thisne!"—"Ah,
Pyramus, my lover dear, thy Thisbe dear and lady dear!"

QUINCE
45   No, no. You must play Pyramus.—And Flute, you Thisbe.

BOTTOM
Well, proceed.

QUINCE
Robin Starveling, the tailor?

STARVELING
Here, Peter Quince.

QUINCE
Robin Starveling, you must play Thisbe's mother.—Tom
50   Snout, the tinker?

SNOUT
Here, Peter Quince.

QUINCE
You, Pyramus' father.—Myself, Thisbe's father.—Snug
the joiner, you, the lion's part.—And I hope here is a play
fitted.

FLUTE

Who's Thisbe? A knight on a quest?

QUINCE

Thisbe is the lady Pyramus is in love with.

FLUTE

No, come on, don't make me play a woman. I'm growing a beard.

QUINCE

That doesn't matter. You'll wear a mask, and you can
make your voice as high as you want to.

BOTTOM

In that case, if I can wear a mask, let me play Thisbe
too! I'll be Pyramus first: "Thisne, Thisne!"—And
then in falsetto: "Ah, Pyramus, my dear lover! I'm
your dear Thisbe, your dear lady!"

QUINCE

No, no. Bottom, you're Pyramus.—And Flute,
you're Thisbe.

BOTTOM

All right. Go on.

QUINCE

Robin Starveling, the tailor?

STARVELING

Here, Peter Quince.

QUINCE

Robin Starveling, you're going to play Thisbe's
mother.—Tom Snout, the handyman.

SNOUT

Here, Peter Quince.

QUINCE

You'll be Pyramus's father—I'll play Thisbe's father
myself—Snug, the cabinetmaker, you'll play the part
of the lion.—So that's everyone. I hope this play is
well cast now.

SNUG
55   Have you the lion's part written? Pray you, if it be, give it
       me, for I am slow of study.

QUINCE
       You may do it extempore, for it is nothing but roaring.

BOTTOM
       Let me play the lion too. I will roar, that I will do any man's
       heart good to hear me. I will roar, that I will make the duke
60   say, "Let him roar again. Let him roar again."

QUINCE
       An you should do it too terribly, you would fright the
       duchess and the ladies, that they would shriek. And that
       were enough to hang us all.

ALL
       That would hang us, every mother's son.

BOTTOM
65   I grant you, friends, if you should fright the ladies out of
       their wits, they would have no more discretion but to hang
       us. But I will aggravate my voice so that I will roar you as
       gently as any sucking dove. I will roar you an 'twere any
       nightingale.

QUINCE
70   You can play no part but Pyramus. For Pyramus is a sweet-
       faced man, a proper man as one shall see in a summer's day,
       a most lovely, gentlemanlike man. Therefore you must
       needs play Pyramus.

BOTTOM
       Well, I will undertake it. What beard were I best to play it
75   in?

QUINCE
       Why, what you will.

SNUG

Do you have the lion's part written down? If you do, please give it to me, because I need to start learning the lines. It takes me a long time to learn things.

QUINCE

You can improvise the whole thing. It's just roaring.

BOTTOM

Let me play the lion too. I'll roar so well that it'll be an inspiration to anyone who hears me. I'll roar so well that the duke will say, "Let him roar again. Let him roar again."

QUINCE

If you roar too ferociously, you'll scare the duchess and the other ladies and make them scream. And that would get us all executed.

ALL

Yeah, that would get every single one of us executed.

BOTTOM

Well, my friends, you've got to admit that if you scare the living daylights out of the ladies, they'd have no choice but to execute us. But I'll soften my voice—you know, aggravate it, so to speak—so that I'll roar as gently as a baby dove. I'll roar like a sweet, peaceful nightingale.

"Aggravate" is a mistake for "moderate."

QUINCE

You can't play any part except Pyramus. Because Pyramus is a good-looking man, the most handsome man that you could find on a summer's day, a lovely gentlemanly man. So you're the only one who could play Pyramus.

BOTTOM

Well then, I'll do it. What kind of beard should I wear for the part?

QUINCE

Whatever kind you want, I guess.

BOTTOM

I will discharge it in either your straw-color beard, your orange-tawny beard, your purple-in-grain beard, or your French crown-color beard, your perfect yellow.

QUINCE

80   Some of your French crowns have no hair at all, and then you will play barefaced.—But masters, here are your parts. And I am to entreat you, request you, and desire you to con them by tomorrow night and meet me in the palace wood, a mile without the town, by moonlight. There will we
85   rehearse, for if we meet in the city we shall be dogged with company, and our devices known. In the meantime I will draw a bill of properties such as our play wants. I pray you, fail me not.

BOTTOM

We will meet, and there we may rehearse most obscenely
90   and courageously. Take pains. Be perfect. Adieu.

QUINCE

At the duke's oak we meet.

BOTTOM

Enough. Hold, or cut bowstrings.

Exeunt

BOTTOM

I'll play the part wearing either a straw-colored beard, or a sandy beard, or a red beard, or one of those bright yellow beards that's the color of a French coin.

QUINCE

Some French people don't have beards at all, because syphilis has made all their hair fall out, so you might have to play the part clean-shaven.—But gentlemen, here are your scripts, and I beg you to please learn them by tomorrow night. Meet me in the duke's forest a mile outside of town. It's best to rehearse there, because if we do it here in the city, we'll be bothered by crowds of people and everyone will know the plot of our play. Meanwhile, I'll make a list of props that we'll need for the play. Now make sure you show up, all of you. Don't leave me in the lurch.

BOTTOM

We'll be there, and there we'll rehearse courageously and wonderfully, truly obscenely. Work hard, know your lines. Goodbye.

QUINCE

We'll meet at the giant oak tree in the duke's forest.

BOTTOM

Got it? Be there, or don't show your face again.

They all exit.

ACT TWO

Scene 1

Enter a FAIRY *at one side and* ROBIN *(*ROBIN GOODFELLOW*) at another*

ROBIN
How now, spirit? Whither wander you?

FAIRY
    Over hill, over dale,
    Thorough bush, thorough brier,
    Over park, over pale,
5   Thorough flood, thorough fire.
    I do wander everywhere
    Swifter than the moon's sphere.
    And I serve the fairy queen
    To dew her orbs upon the green.
10   The cowslips tall her pensioners be.
    In their gold coats spots you see.
    Those be rubies, fairy favors.
    In those freckles live their savors.
    I must go seek some dewdrops here
15   And hang a pearl in every cowslip's ear.
Farewell, thou lob of spirits. I'll be gone.
Our queen and all our elves come here anon.

ROBIN
The king doth keep his revels here tonight.
Take heed the queen come not within his sight.
20 For Oberon is passing fell and wrath
Because that she, as her attendant hath
A lovely boy stolen from an Indian king.
She never had so sweet a changeling.
And jealous Oberon would have the child
25 Knight of his train, to trace the forests wild.
But she perforce withholds the lovèd boy,
Crowns him with flowers, and makes him all her joy.

ACT TWO

Scene 1

A FAIRY *and* ROBIN GOODFELLOW *(a "puck" or mischievous spirit) meet onstage.*

ROBIN

Hello, spirit! Where are you going?

FAIRY

I go over hills and valleys, through bushes and thorns, over parks and fenced-in spaces, through water and fire. I wander everywhere faster than the moon revolves around the Earth. I work for Titania, the Fairy Queen, and organize fairy dances for her in the grass. The cowslip flowers are her bodyguards. You'll see that their petals have spots on them—those are rubies, fairy gifts. Their sweet smells come from those little freckles. Now I have to go find some dewdrops and hang a pearl earring on every cowslip flower. Goodbye, you dumb old spirit. I've got to go. The queen and her elves will be here soon.

ROBIN

The king's having a party here tonight. Just make sure the queen doesn't come anywhere near him, because King Oberon is extremely angry. He's furious because she stole an adorable boy from an Indian king. She's never kidnapped such a darling human child before, and Oberon's jealous. He wants the child for himself, to accompany him on his wanderings through the wild forests. But the queen refuses to hand the boy over to Oberon. Instead, she puts flowers in the boy's hair and makes a fuss over him. And now Oberon and Titania refuse to speak to each other, or meet each

And now they never meet in grove or green,
By fountain clear or spangled starlight sheen.
30 But they do square, that all their elves for fear
Creep into acorn cups and hide them there.

FAIRY

Either I mistake your shape and making quite,
Or else you are that shrewd and knavish sprite
Called Robin Goodfellow. Are not you he
35 That frights the maidens of the villagery,
Skim milk, and sometimes labor in the quern
And bootless make the breathless housewife churn,
And sometime make the drink to bear no barm,
Mislead night-wanderers, laughing at their harm?
40 Those that "Hobgoblin" call you, and "sweet Puck,"
You do their work, and they shall have good luck.
Are not you he?

ROBIN

                    Thou speak'st aright.
I am that merry wanderer of the night.
I jest to Oberon and make him smile
45 When I a fat and bean-fed horse beguile,
Neighing in likeness of a filly foal.
And sometime lurk I in a gossip's bowl
In very likeness of a roasted crab,
And when she drinks, against her lips I bob
50 And on her withered dewlap pour the ale.
The wisest aunt telling the saddest tale
Sometime for three-foot stool mistaketh me.
Then slip I from her bum, down topples she,
And "Tailor!" cries, and falls into a cough,
55 And then the whole quire hold their hips and laugh,
And waxen in their mirth, and neeze, and swear
A merrier hour was never wasted there.
But, room, fairy! Here comes Oberon.

FAIRY

And here my mistress. Would that he were gone!

other anywhere—neither in the forest nor on the plain, nor by the river nor under the stars. They always argue, and the little fairies get so frightened that they hide in acorn cups and won't come out.

FAIRY

Unless I'm mistaken, you're that mischievous and naughty spirit named Robin Goodfellow. Aren't you the one who goes around scaring the maidens in the village, stealing the cream from the top of the milk, screwing up the flour mills, and frustrating house-wives by keeping their milk from turning into butter? Aren't you the one who keeps beer from foaming up as it should, and causes people to get lost at night, while you laugh at them? Some people call you "Hobgob-lin" and "sweet Puck," and you're nice to them. You do their work for them and give them good luck. That's you, right?

ROBIN

What you say is true. That's me you're talking about, the playful wanderer of the night. I tell jokes to Oberon and make him smile. I'll trick a fat, well-fed horse into thinking that I'm a young female horse. Sometimes I hide at the bottom of an old woman's drink disguised as an apple. When she takes a sip, I bob up against her lips and make her spill the drink all over her withered old neck. Sometimes a wise old woman with a sad story to tell tries to sit down on me, thinking I'm a three-legged stool. But I slip from underneath her and she falls down, crying, "Ow, my butt!" and starts coughing, and then everyone laughs and has fun. But step aside, fairy! Here comes Oberon.

FAIRY

And here's my mistress, Titania. I wish he'd go away!

Enter OBERON, *the King of Fairies, at one side with his train, and* TITANIA, *the Queen, at the other, with hers*

OBERON

60   Ill met by moonlight, proud Titania.

TITANIA

What, jealous Oberon?—Fairies, skip hence.
I have forsworn his bed and company.

OBERON

Tarry, rash wanton. Am not I thy lord?

TITANIA

Then I must be thy lady. But I know
65   When thou hast stolen away from Fairyland,
And in the shape of Corin sat all day,
Playing on pipes of corn and versing love
To amorous Phillida. Why art thou here,
Come from the farthest step of India?
70   But that, forsooth, the bouncing Amazon,
Your buskined mistress and your warrior love,
To Theseus must be wedded, and you come
To give their bed joy and prosperity.

OBERON

How canst thou thus for shame, Titania,
75   Glance at my credit with Hippolyta,
Knowing I know thy love to Theseus?
Didst thou not lead him through the glimmering night
From Perigouna, whom he ravishèd?
And make him with fair Ægles break his faith,
80   With Ariadne and Antiopa?

TITANIA

These are the forgeries of jealousy.
And never, since the middle summer's spring,
Met we on hill, in dale, forest, or mead,

OBERON, *the Fairy King, and his followers enter. On the opposite side of the stage,* TITANIA, *the Fairy Queen, and her followers enter.*

OBERON

How *not* nice to see you, Titania.

TITANIA

What, are you jealous, Oberon?—Fairies, let's get out of here. I've sworn I'll never sleep with him or talk to him again.

OBERON

Wait just a minute, you brazen hussy. Aren't you supposed to obey me, your lord and husband?

TITANIA

If you're my lord and husband, I must be your lady and wife, so you're supposed to be faithful to me. But I know for a fact that you snuck away from Fairyland disguised as a shepherd, and spent all day playing straw pipes and singing love poems to your new girlfriend. The only reason you left India was to come here and see that butch Amazon Hippolyta. She was your boot-wearing mistress and your warrior lover, and now that she's getting married to Theseus, you've come to celebrate their marriage.

OBERON

How can you stand there shamelessly talking about me and Hippolyta, when you know that I know about your love for Theseus? Weren't you the one who made him desert Perigouna in the middle of the night, right after he'd raped her? And weren't you the one who made him cheat on all of his other girlfriends, like Aegles, Ariadne, and Antiopa?

TITANIA

These are nothing but jealous lies. Since the beginning of midsummer, my fairies and I haven't been able to meet anywhere to do our dances in the wind without being disturbed by you and your arguments.

By pavèd fountain, or by rushy brook,
85   Or in the beachèd margent of the sea,
To dance our ringlets to the whistling wind,
But with thy brawls thou hast disturbed our sport.
Therefore the winds, piping to us in vain,
As in revenge, have sucked up from the sea
90   Contagious fogs, which falling in the land
Have every pelting river made so proud
That they have overborne their continents.
The ox hath therefore stretched his yoke in vain,
The ploughman lost his sweat, and the green corn
95   Hath rotted ere his youth attained a beard.
The fold stands empty in the drownèd field,
And crows are fatted with the murrain flock.
The nine-men's-morris is filled up with mud,
And the quaint mazes in the wanton green
100   For lack of tread are undistinguishable.
The human mortals want their winter here.
No night is now with hymn or carol blessed.
Therefore the moon, the governess of floods,
Pale in her anger, washes all the air,
105   That rheumatic diseases do abound.
And thorough this distemperature we see
The seasons alter: hoary-headed frosts
Fall in the fresh lap of the crimson rose,
And on old Hiems' thin and icy crown
110   An odorous chaplet of sweet summer buds
Is, as in mockery, set. The spring, the summer,
The childing autumn, angry winter change
Their wonted liveries, and the mazèd world,
By their increase, now knows not which is which.
115   And this same progeny of evils comes
From our debate, from our dissension.
We are their parents and original.

We haven't been able to meet on a hill or in a valley, in the forest or a meadow, by a pebbly fountain or a rushing stream, or on the beach by the ocean without you disturbing us. And because you interrupt us so that we can't dance for them, the winds have made fogs rise up out of the sea and fall down on the rivers so that the rivers flood, just to get revenge on you. So all the work that oxen and farmers have done in plowing the fields has been for nothing, because the unripe grain has rotted before it was ripe. Sheep pens are empty in the middle of the flooded fields, and the crows get fat from eating the dead bodies of infected sheep. All the fields where people usually play games are filled with mud, and you can't even see the elaborate mazes that people create in the grass, because no one walks in them anymore and they've all grown over. It's not winter here for the human mortals, so they're not protected by the holy hymns and carols that they sing in winter. So the pale, angry moon, who controls the tides, fills the air with diseases. As a consequence of this bad weather and these bad moods the seasons have started to change. Cold frosts spread over the red roses, and the icy winter wears a crown of sweet summer flowers as some sick joke. Spring, summer, fertile autumn and angry winter have all changed places, and now the confused world doesn't know which is which. And this is all because of our argument. We are responsible for this.

OBERON
Do you amend it then. It lies in you.
Why should Titania cross her Oberon?
120 I do but beg a little changeling boy,
To be my henchman.

TITANIA
Set your heart at rest.
The Fairyland buys not the child of me.
His mother was a votaress of my order,
And in the spicèd Indian air by night
125 Full often hath she gossiped by my side,
And sat with me on Neptune's yellow sands,
Marking th' embarkèd traders on the flood,
When we have laughed to see the sails conceive
And grow big-bellied with the wanton wind;
130 Which she, with pretty and with swimming gait
Following—her womb then rich with my young squire—
Would imitate, and sail upon the land
To fetch me trifles and return again
As from a voyage, rich with merchandise.
135 But she, being mortal, of that boy did die.
And for her sake do I rear up her boy,
And for her sake I will not part with him.

OBERON
How long within this wood intend you stay?

TITANIA
Perchance till after Theseus' wedding day.
140 If you will patiently dance in our round
And see our moonlight revels, go with us.
If not, shun me, and I will spare your haunts.

OBERON
Give me that boy and I will go with thee.

TITANIA
Not for thy fairy kingdom.—Fairies, away!
145 We shall chide downright, if I longer stay.

Exeunt TITANIA *and her train*

OBERON

Do something about it, then. You have the power to fix it. Why would Titania want to argue with her Oberon? All I'm asking for is to have that little human boy as part of my crew.

TITANIA

Get over it. I won't give up this child for all of Fairyland. His mother was one of my worshippers, and we always used to gossip together at night in India, sitting together by the ocean and watching the merchant ships sailing on the ocean. We used to laugh to see the sails fill up with wind so that they looked like they had big, pregnant bellies, as if the wind had gotten them pregnant. She would imitate them—since she was already pregnant with the little boy—and she would go sailing over the land herself to go get me little presents, and come back carrying gifts like she was a ship coming back from a voyage. But since she was a mortal, she died giving birth to that boy, and for her sake I'm raising him and will not give him up.

OBERON

How long do you plan to stay here in this forest?

TITANIA

Maybe until after Theseus's wedding day. If you behave yourself and join us in our circle dance and moonlight celebrations, then you can come with us. If not, leave me alone, and I'll stay away from your turf.

OBERON

Give me that boy and I'll come with you.

TITANIA

Not for your entire fairy kingdom.—Come, fairies, let's go. We're going to have an out-and-out brawl if I stay any longer.

> TITANIA *and her* FAIRIES *exit.*

OBERON
Well, go thy way. Thou shalt not from this grove
Till I torment thee for this injury.—*(to* **ROBIN GOODFELLOW***)*
My gentle Puck, come hither. Thou rememberest
Since once I sat upon a promontory
150   And heard a mermaid on a dolphin's back
Uttering such dulcet and harmonious breath
That the rude sea grew civil at her song
And certain stars shot madly from their spheres
To hear the seamaid's music?

ROBIN
                                        I remember.

OBERON
155   That very time I saw (but thou couldst not)
Flying between the cold moon and the Earth,
Cupid all armed. A certain aim he took
At a fair vestal thronèd by the west,
And loosed his love shaft smartly from his bow
160   As it should pierce a hundred thousand hearts.
But I might see young Cupid's fiery shaft
Quenched in the chaste beams of the watery moon,
And the imperial votaress passèd on,
In maiden meditation, fancy-free.
165   Yet marked I where the bolt of Cupid fell.
It fell upon a little western flower,
Before milk-white, now purple with love's wound.
And maidens call it "love-in-idleness."
Fetch me that flower. The herb I showed thee once.
170   The juice of it on sleeping eyelids laid
Will make or man or woman madly dote
Upon the next live creature that it sees.
Fetch me this herb, and be thou here again
Ere the leviathan can swim a league.

ROBIN
175   I'll put a girdle round about the Earth
In forty minutes.

OBERON

Well, go on your way, then. You won't leave this grove until I've paid you back for this insult. *(to* ROBIN GOOD-FELLOW*)* My dear Puck, come here. You remember the time when I was sitting on a cliff, and I heard a mermaid sitting on a dolphin's back sing such a sweet and harmonious song that it calmed the stormy sea and made stars shoot out of the sky so they could hear her better?

ROBIN

Yes, I remember.

OBERON

That same night, I saw Cupid flying from the moon to the earth, with all of his arrows ready. (You couldn't see him, but I could.) He took aim at a beautiful young virgin who was sitting on a throne in the western part of the world, and he shot his arrow of love well enough to have pierced a hundred thousand hearts. But I could see that Cupid's fiery arrow was put out by watery, virginal moonbeams, so the royal virgin continued her virginal thoughts without being interrupted by thoughts of love. But I paid attention to where Cupid's arrow fell. It fell on a little western flower, which used to be white as milk but now has turned purple from being wounded by the arrow of love. Young girls call it "love-in-idleness." Bring me that flower. I showed it to you once. If its juice is put on someone's eyelids while they're asleep, that person will fall in love with the next living creature he or she sees. Bring me this plant, and get back here before the sea monster has time to swim three miles.

ROBIN

I could go around the world in forty minutes.

Exit ROBIN

OBERON
                    Having once this juice,
I'll watch Titania when she is asleep
And drop the liquor of it in her eyes.
The next thing then she waking looks upon—
180   Be it on lion, bear, or wolf, or bull,
On meddling monkey or on busy ape—
She shall pursue it with the soul of love.
And ere I take this charm from of her sight—
As I can take it with another herb—
185   I'll make her render up her page to me.
But who comes here? I am invisible.
And I will overhear their conference.

Enter DEMETRIUS, HELENA *following him*

DEMETRIUS
I love thee not, therefore pursue me not.
Where is Lysander and fair Hermia?
190   The one I'll stay, the other stayeth me.
Thou told'st me they were stol'n unto this wood.
And here am I, and wood within this wood,
Because I cannot meet my Hermia.
Hence, get thee gone, and follow me no more.

HELENA
195   You draw me, you hard-hearted adamant.
But yet you draw not iron, for my heart
Is true as steel. Leave you your power to draw,
And I shall have no power to follow you.

DEMETRIUS
Do I entice you? Do I speak you fair?
200   Or rather, do I not in plainest truth
Tell you I do not, nor I cannot, love you?

ROBIN *exits.*

OBERON

When I have the juice of that flower, I'll trickle some drops of it on Titania's eyes while she's sleeping. She'll fall madly in love with the first thing she sees when she wakes up—even if it's a lion, a bear, a wolf, a bull, a monkey, or an ape. And before I make her normal again—I can cure her by treating her with another plant—I'll make her give me that little boy as my page. But who's that coming this way? I'll make myself invisible and listen to their conversation.

DEMETRIUS *enters, followed by* HELENA.

DEMETRIUS

Look, I don't love you, so stop following me around. Where are Lysander and beautiful Hermia? Lysander I want to stop, but Hermia stops my heart from beating. You told me they escaped into this forest. And here I am, going crazy in the middle of the woods because I can't find my Hermia. Go away, get out of here, and stop following me.

HELENA

You attract me to you, you cruel magnet! But you must not attract iron, because my heart is as true as steel. If you let go of your power to attract me, I won't have any power to follow you.

DEMETRIUS

Do I ask you to follow me? Do I speak to you kindly? Don't I tell you in the clearest terms that I do not and cannot love you?

ACT TWO

HELENA
And even for that do I love you the more.
I am your spaniel. And, Demetrius,
The more you beat me, I will fawn on you.
205 Use me but as your spaniel—spurn me, strike me,
Neglect me, lose me. Only give me leave,
Unworthy as I am, to follow you.
What worser place can I beg in your love—
And yet a place of high respect with me—
210 Than to be usèd as you use your dog?

DEMETRIUS
Tempt not too much the hatred of my spirit.
For I am sick when I do look on thee.

HELENA
And I am sick when I look not on you.

DEMETRIUS
You do impeach your modesty too much,
215 To leave the city and commit yourself
Into the hands of one that loves you not,
To trust the opportunity of night
And the ill counsel of a desert place
With the rich worth of your virginity.

HELENA
220 Your virtue is my privilege. For that
It is not night when I do see your face.
Therefore I think I am not in the night.
Nor doth this wood lack worlds of company,
For you in my respect are all the world.
225 Then how can it be said I am alone
When all the world is here to look on me?

DEMETRIUS
I'll run from thee and hide me in the brakes,
And leave thee to the mercy of wild beasts.

HELENA
The wildest hath not such a heart as you.
230 Run when you will, the story shall be changed.

HELENA

Yes, but that makes me love you even more. I'm your little dog, Demetrius. The more you beat me, the more I'll love you. Treat me like you would treat a dog—kick me, hit me, neglect me, try to lose me. Just let me follow behind you, even though I'm not good enough for you. Could I ask for a worse place in your heart than to be treated as you would treat a dog? And yet I would consider it an honor to be your dog.

DEMETRIUS

Don't push it. Just looking at you makes me sick.

HELENA

And I get sick when I can't look at you.

DEMETRIUS

You're risking your reputation by leaving the city and stalking someone who doesn't love you. Standing around alone in a deserted area in the middle of the night isn't the best way to protect your virginity.

HELENA

I rely on your virtue to protect me. And because I can see your shining face, it doesn't feel like nighttime to me. This forest doesn't seem deserted when you're here, because you are all the world to me. So how can anyone say I'm alone, when the whole world is here to look at me?

DEMETRIUS

I'll run away from you and hide in the bushes, and leave you to the mercy of wild animals.

HELENA

The wildest animal isn't as cruel as you are. Run whenever you want to. The story of Daphne and Apollo will be changed: the lustful god Apollo runs

Apollo flies and Daphne holds the chase.
The dove pursues the griffin. The mild hind
Makes speed to catch the tiger—bootless speed,
When cowardice pursues and valor flies.

DEMETRIUS

235   I will not stay thy questions. Let me go.
Or if thou follow me, do not believe
But I shall do thee mischief in the wood.

HELENA

Ay, in the temple, in the town, the field
You do me mischief. Fie, Demetrius!
240   Your wrongs do set a scandal on my sex.
We cannot fight for love as men may do.
We should be wooed and were not made to woo.

Exit DEMETRIUS

I'll follow thee and make a heaven of hell,
To die upon the hand I love so well.

Exit HELENA

OBERON

245   Fare thee well, nymph. Ere he do leave this grove,
Thou shalt fly him and he shall seek thy love.

Enter ROBIN

Hast thou the flower there? Welcome, wanderer.

ROBIN

Ay, there it is.

OBERON

                 I pray thee, give it me.
(takes flower from ROBIN*)*
I know a bank where the wild thyme blows,
250   Where oxlips and the nodding violet grows,
Quite overcanopied with luscious woodbine,
With sweet musk roses and with eglantine.
There sleeps Titania sometime of the night,

away from the virginal nymph Daphne who pursues him, the dove chases after the griffin, which is usually its predator, and the gentle deer tries to hunt down the tiger—speed is useless when the cowardly person chases and the brave person runs away.

DEMETRIUS

I'm not sticking around to listen to you any longer. Leave me alone. Or if you follow me, you'd better understand that I'll do something bad to you in the forest.

HELENA

Yes, you already hurt me in the church, in the town, and in the fields. Shame on you, Demetrius! Your behavior is an insult to all women. We cannot fight for love as men can. We should be pursued and courted. We weren't made to do the pursuing.

DEMETRIUS exits.

I'll follow you and turn this hell I'm in into a kind of heaven. It would be heavenly to be killed by someone I love so much.

HELENA exits.

OBERON

Goodbye, nymph. Before he leaves this part of the forest, you'll change places: you'll be the one running away, and he'll be in love with you.

ROBIN *enters.*

Do you have the flower? Welcome, traveler.

ROBIN

Yes, here it is.

OBERON

Please, give it to me. *(he takes the flower from* ROBIN*)* I know a place where wild thyme blooms, and oxlips and violets grow. It's covered over with luscious hon-

Lulled in these flowers with dances and delight.
255 And there the snake throws her enameled skin,
Weed wide enough to wrap a fairy in.
And with the juice of this I'll streak her eyes
And make her full of hateful fantasies.
(gives ROBIN *some of the flower)*
Take thou some of it and seek through this grove:
260 A sweet Athenian lady is in love
With a disdainful youth. Anoint his eyes.
But do it when the next thing he espies
May be the lady. Thou shalt know the man
By the Athenian garments he hath on.
265 Effect it with some care, that he may prove
More fond on her than she upon her love.
And look thou meet me ere the first cock crow.

ROBIN
Fear not, my lord. Your servant shall do so.

Exeunt severally

eysuckle, sweet muskroses and sweetbrier. Titania sleeps there sometimes at night, lulled to sleep among the flowers by dances and other delights. Snakes shed their skin there, and the shed skin is wide enough to wrap a fairy in. I'll put the juice of this flower on Titania's eyes, and fill her with horrible delusions and desires. *(he gives* ROBIN *part of the flower)* You take some of it too, and look around in this part of the forest. A sweet Athenian lady is in love with a young man who wants nothing to do with her. Put some of this flower's juice on his eyes, and make sure to do it in such a way that the next thing he sees will be the lady. You'll be able to tell it's him because he's wearing Athenian clothes. Do it carefully, so that he'll end up loving her more than she loves him. And then make sure to meet me before the rooster's first crow at dawn.

ROBIN

Don't worry, sir. I'm at your service.

They all exit, separately.

ACT TWO, Scene 2

Enter TITANIA, *Queen of Fairies, with her train of* FAIRIES

TITANIA
Come now, a roundel and a fairy song.
Then for the third part of a minute, hence—
Some to kill cankers in the musk-rose buds,
Some war with reremice for their leathern wings
5 To make my small elves coats, and some keep back
The clamorous owl that nightly hoots and wonders
At our quaint spirits. Sing me now asleep.
Then to your offices and let me rest.

FAIRIES *sing*

FIRST FAIRY
(sings)
You spotted snakes with double tongue,
10 Thorny hedgehogs, be not seen.
Newts and blindworms, do no wrong.
Come not near our fairy queen.

FAIRIES
(sing)
Philomel, with melody
Sing in our sweet lullaby.
15 Lulla, lulla, lullaby, lulla, lulla, lullaby.
Never harm
Nor spell nor charm
Come our lovely lady nigh.
So good night, with lullaby.

FIRST FAIRY
(sings)
20 Weaving spiders, come not here.
Hence, you long-legged spinners, hence!

ACT TWO, Scene 2

TITANIA, *the Fairy Queen, enters with her following of*
FAIRIES.

TITANIA

Come, dance in a circle and sing a fairy song, and then
go off for a while to do your work. Some of you will kill
the worms infesting the rosebuds, some of you will
fight with bats to get their leathery wings, so we can
make coats for my small elves. Some of you will keep
that loud owl away, the one that hoots and wonders
every night at us dainty fairies. Sing me to sleep now,
and then go off to do your duties and let me rest.

The FAIRIES *sing.*

FIRST FAIRY
(*singing*)
> Snakes with forked tongues,
> And porcupines, don't be seen.
> Deadly lizards, don't be mean.
> Don't come near our fairy queen.

FAIRIES
(*singing*)
> Nightingale, melodiously
> Sing our sweet lullaby.
> Lulla, lulla, lullaby, lulla, lulla, lullaby.
> Let no harm
> Or spell or charm
> Come near our lovely lady.
> Say good night with a lullaby.

FIRST FAIRY
(*singing*)
> Spiders with your webs, stay away.
> You long-legged things, begone!

ACT TWO

Beetles black, approach not near.
Worm nor snail, do no offense.

FAIRIES
(sing)

Philomel, with melody
25   Sing in our sweet lullaby.
Lulla, lulla, lullaby, lulla, lulla, lullaby.
Never harm
Nor spell nor charm
Come our lovely lady nigh.
30   So good night, with lullaby.

TITANIA *sleeps*

SECOND FAIRY
Hence, away! Now all is well.
One aloof stand sentinel.

Exeunt **FAIRIES**

Enter **OBERON**

OBERON
(squeezing flower juice on **TITANIA** *'s eyelids)*
What thou seest when thou dost wake,
Do it for thy true love take.
35   Love and languish for his sake.
Be it ounce or cat or bear,
Pard or boar with bristled hair,
In thy eye that shall appear,
When thou wakest, it is thy dear.
40   Wake when some vile thing is near.

Exit **OBERON**

Enter **LYSANDER** *and* **HERMIA**

LYSANDER
Fair love, you faint with wandering in the wood.
And to speak troth, I have forgot our way.

> *Black beetles, don't come near.*
> *Worms and snails, don't be bad.*

FAIRIES
> *(singing)*
> > *Nightingale, melodiously*
> > *Sing our sweet lullaby.*
> > *Lulla, lulla, lullaby, lulla, lulla, lullaby.*
> > *Let no harm*
> > *Or spell or charm*
> > *Come near our lovely lady.*
> > *Say good night with a lullaby.*

> **TITANIA** *falls asleep.*

SECOND FAIRY
> Okay, let's go! Everything's fine now. One of us will stay and stand guard.
> > *The* **FAIRIES** *exit.*
>
> **OBERON** *enters.*

OBERON
> *(he squeezes flower juice on* **TITANIA**'s *eyelids)*
> Whatever you see first when you wake up, think of it as your true love. Love him and yearn for him, even if he's a lynx, a cat, a bear, a leopard, or a wild boar. Whatever's there when you wake up will be dear to you. Wake up when something nasty is nearby.

> > **OBERON** *exits.*
>
> **LYSANDER** *and* **HERMIA** *enter.*

LYSANDER
> My love, you look like you're about to faint from wandering in the woods for so long, and to tell you the truth, I've gotten us lost. We'll take a rest, if you think

We'll rest us, Hermia, if you think it good.
And tarry for the comfort of the day.

HERMIA
45   Be it so, Lysander. Find you out a bed,
For I upon this bank will rest my head.

LYSANDER
One turf shall serve as pillow for us both.
One heart, one bed, two bosoms, and one troth.

HERMIA
Nay, good Lysander. For my sake, my dear,
50   Lie further off yet. Do not lie so near.

LYSANDER
O, take the sense, sweet, of my innocence.
Love takes the meaning in love's conference.
I mean that my heart unto yours is knit
So that but one heart we can make of it.
55   Two bosoms interchainèd with an oath—
So then two bosoms and a single troth.
Then by your side no bed room me deny.
For, lying so, Hermia, I do not lie.

HERMIA
Lysander riddles very prettily.
60   Now much beshrew my manners and my pride
If Hermia meant to say Lysander lied.
But, gentle friend, for love and courtesy
Lie further off in human modesty.
Such separation as may well be said
65   Becomes a virtuous bachelor and a maid.
So far be distant. And, good night, sweet friend.
Thy love ne'er alter till thy sweet life end!

LYSANDER
Amen, amen to that fair prayer, say I.
And then end life when I end loyalty!
70   Here is my bed. Sleep give thee all his rest!

it's a good idea, and wait until daylight when things will be easier.

HERMIA

Let's do that, Lysander. Find something to cushion you while you sleep. I'm going to rest my head on this little slope.

LYSANDER

We can both sleep together on the grass. We'll have one heart, one bed, two bodies, and one faithful vow.

HERMIA

No, Lysander. Please, for my sake, sleep a little farther away. Don't sleep so close to me.

LYSANDER

Oh, sweetheart, I didn't mean anything naughty when I said that. When lovers talk to each other, their hearts should understand each other. I just meant that our hearts are joined, so we can almost think of them as one heart. Our two bodies are linked together by the promises we've made to each other, so there are two bodies and one faithful vow. So let me sleep next to you. If I lie *next* to you, I won't lie *to* you—I'll be faithful and respect you.

HERMIA

Lysander's got a way with words. I would certainly be rude and shameful if I had implied that you were a liar. But please, darling, sleep a little farther away so we can behave properly. It's only proper for a well-behaved bachelor and a well-behaved girl to be physically separated like this. Stay away for now, and good night, my sweet friend. I hope your love for me remains this strong for your entire life!

LYSANDER

Amen to that. I hope my life ends before my loyalty to you does. I'll sleep over here. Sleep well!

HERMIA
With half that wish the wisher's eyes be pressed!

HERMIA and LYSANDER sleep
Enter ROBIN

ROBIN
Through the forest have I gone.
But Athenian found I none,
On whose eyes I might approve
This flower's force in stirring love.
(sees LYSANDER and HERMIA)
Night and silence! Who is here?
Weeds of Athens he doth wear.
This is he, my master said,
Despisèd the Athenian maid.
And here the maiden, sleeping sound
On the dank and dirty ground.
Pretty soul! She durst not lie
Near this lack-love, this kill-courtesy.
(squeezes flower juice on LYSANDER's eyelids)
Churl, upon thy eyes I throw
All the power this charm doth owe.
When thou wakest, let love forbid
Sleep his seat on thy eyelid.
So awake when I am gone,
For I must now to Oberon.

Exit ROBIN

Enter DEMETRIUS and HELENA, running

HELENA
Stay, though thou kill me, sweet Demetrius.
DEMETRIUS
I charge thee, hence, and do not haunt me thus.
HELENA
O, wilt thou darkling leave me? Do not so.

HERMIA

You sleep well too.

HERMIA *and* LYSANDER *sleep.* ROBIN *enters.*

ROBIN

I've been through the entire forest, but I haven't found any Athenian man to use the flower on. *(he sees* LYSANDER *and* HERMIA*)* Wait a second, who's this? He's wearing Athenian clothes. This must be the guy who rejected the Athenian girl. And here's the girl, sleeping soundly on the damp and dirty ground. Pretty girl! She shouldn't lie near this rude and heartless man. *(he puts flower juice on* LYSANDER*'s eyelids)* Jerk, I throw all the power of this magic charm on your eyes. When you wake up, let love keep you from going back to sleep. Wake up when I'm gone, because now I have to go to Oberon.

ROBIN *exits.*

DEMETRIUS *and* HELENA *enter, running.*

HELENA

Stop, Demetrius! Stop, even if only to kill me.

DEMETRIUS

I'm telling you, get out of here, and don't follow me around like this.

HELENA

Oh, will you leave me alone in the dark? Don't.

ACT TWO

DEMETRIUS
Stay, on thy peril. I alone will go.

Exit DEMETRIUS

HELENA
Oh, I am out of breath in this fond chase.
95 The more my prayer, the lesser is my grace.
Happy is Hermia, wheresoe'er she lies,
For she hath blessèd and attractive eyes.
How came her eyes so bright? Not with salt tears.
If so, my eyes are oftener washed than hers.
100 No, no, I am as ugly as a bear,
For beasts that meet me run away for fear.
Therefore no marvel though Demetrius
Do, as a monster, fly my presence thus.
What wicked and dissembling glass of mine
105 Made me compare with Hermia's sphery eyne?
(sees LYSANDER*)* But who is here? Lysander, on the ground?
Dead or asleep? I see no blood, no wound.—
Lysander, if you live, good sir, awake.

LYSANDER
(waking) And run through fire I will for thy sweet sake.
110 Transparent Helena! Nature shows art
That through thy bosom makes me see thy heart.
Where is Demetrius? Oh, how fit a word
Is that vile name to perish on my sword!

HELENA
Do not say so, Lysander. Say not so.
115 What though he love your Hermia? Lord, what though?
Yet Hermia still loves you. Then be content.

LYSANDER
Content with Hermia? No. I do repent
The tedious minutes I with her have spent.
Not Hermia but Helena I love.
120 Who will not change a raven for a dove?
The will of man is by his reason swayed,

DEMETRIUS
Stay here at your own risk. I'm going on alone.

DEMETRIUS exits

.

HELENA
Oh, I'm out of breath from this foolish chase. The more I pray, the less I get out of it. Hermia is lucky, wherever she is, because she has beautiful eyes. How did her eyes get so bright? Not from crying. If that's the case, tears wash my eyes more than hers. No, no, I'm as ugly as a bear, since animals that see me run away in terror. So it's no surprise that Demetrius runs away from me as if I were a monster. What evil and deceitful mirror made me think I could rival Hermia's starry eyes? *(she sees* LYSANDER*)* But who's this here? Lysander, on the ground? Is he dead or sleeping? I don't see any blood or injuries—Lysander, if you're alive, wake up.

LYSANDER
(waking up) I'd even run through fire if you told me to. Radiant, beautiful Helena! I feel like Mother Nature has allowed me to see into your heart, as if by magic. Where is Demetrius? Oh, I'd kill that name with my sword if I could!

HELENA
Don't say that, Lysander. Don't say that. Why do you care that he loves Hermia? What does it matter? Hermia still loves you, so be happy.

LYSANDER
Happy with Hermia? No. I regret all the boring time I wasted with her. I don't love Hermia; I love Helena. Who wouldn't love a dove more than a crow? A man's desires are influenced by his logical mind, and it's

And reason says you are the worthier maid.
Things growing are not ripe until their season.
So I, being young, till now ripe not to reason.
125   And touching now the point of human skill,
Reason becomes the marshal to my will
And leads me to your eyes, where I o'erlook
Love's stories written in love's richest book.

HELENA
Wherefore was I to this keen mockery born?
130   When at your hands did I deserve this scorn?
Is 't not enough, is 't not enough, young man,
That I did never, no, nor never can,
Deserve a sweet look from Demetrius' eye,
But you must flout my insufficiency?
135   Good troth, you do me wrong, good sooth, you do,
In such disdainful manner me to woo.
But fare you well. Perforce I must confess
I thought you lord of more true gentleness.
Oh, that a lady of one man refused
140   Should of another therefore be abused!

Exit HELENA

LYSANDER
She sees not Hermia.—Hermia, sleep thou there.
And never mayst thou come Lysander near!
For as a surfeit of the sweetest things
The deepest loathing to the stomach brings,
145   Or as the heresies that men do leave
Are hated most of those they did deceive,
So thou, my surfeit and my heresy,
Of all be hated, but the most of me.—
And all my powers, address your love and might
150   To honor Helen and to be her knight.

Exit LYSANDER

simply logical that you're more worthy of love than Hermia is. Fruits and vegetables don't ripen until the right season of the year. Likewise, I'm young, and my sense of reason has just ripened. I can finally see the light. My logic has more control over my desires than it used to, and it's telling me to look into your eyes, where I see every love story ever told.

HELENA

Why does everyone always make fun of me? What have I done to deserve this kind of treatment from you? Is it not enough, is it not enough, young man, that I'll never be pretty enough to get a kind look from Demetrius? Do you have to harp on my inadequacy? My God, it's wrong for you to woo me in such a cruel, disdainful way. But goodbye. I have to tell you, I thought you were a much kinder person than this. Oh, how awful that a lady who's been rejected by one man should therefore be treated horribly by another one!

HELENA *exits.*

LYSANDER

She doesn't see Hermia—Hermia, keep sleeping, and don't come near me ever again! Eating too many sweets makes people sick to their stomachs, and people always hate the mistakes they made in the past worse than anyone else hates those mistakes. Hermia, you're the sweet I've had too much of, and the mistake I used to make, so I hate you more than anyone else does.—I'll use all my talents and efforts to serve Helen and bring her honor.

LYSANDER *exits.*

HERMIA

    (waking) Help me, Lysander, help me! Do thy best
    To pluck this crawling serpent from my breast.
    Ay me, for pity! What a dream was here.
    Lysander, look how I do quake with fear.
155   Methought a serpent eat my heart away,
    And you sat smiling at his cruel pray.
    Lysander!—What, removed?—Lysander, lord!—
    What, out of hearing, gone? No sound, no word?—
    Alack, where are you? Speak, an if you hear.
160   Speak, of all loves! I swoon almost with fear.
    No? Then I well perceive you all not nigh.
    Either death or you I'll find immediately.

Exit

HERMIA

(waking up) Help me, Lysander, help me! Get this snake off of my chest. Oh, my God! What a terrible dream I just had! Lysander, look how I'm shaking from fear. I thought a snake was eating my heart while you sat smiling and watching. Lysander!—What, is he gone?—Lysander, my lord!—What, is he out of earshot? Gone? No answer, nothing? Oh, God, where are you? Say something if you can hear me. Say something, please! I'm almost fainting with fear. Nothing? Then I guess you're nowhere nearby. I'll find you—or die—right away.

HERMIA *exits.*

ACT THREE

Scene 1

TITANIA *sleeps. Enter the clowns:* BOTTOM, QUINCE, FLUTE, SNUG, SNOUT, *and* STARVELING

BOTTOM
Are we all met?

QUINCE
Pat, pat. And here's a marvelous convenient place for our rehearsal. This green plot shall be our stage, this hawthorn-brake our tiring-house, and we will do it in action as we will
5 do it before the duke.

BOTTOM
Peter Quince—

QUINCE
What sayest thou, bully Bottom?

BOTTOM
There are things in this comedy of Pyramus and Thisbe that will never please. First, Pyramus must draw a sword to
10 kill himself, which the ladies cannot abide. How answer you that?

SNOUT
By 'r lakin, a parlous fear.

STARVELING
I believe we must leave the killing out, when all is done.

BOTTOM
Not a whit. I have a device to make all well. Write me a
15 prologue, and let the prologue seem to say we will do no harm with our swords, and that Pyramus is not killed indeed. And for the more better assurance, tell them that I, Pyramus, am not Pyramus, but Bottom the weaver. This will put them out of fear.

ACT THREE

Scene 1

While TITANIA *is asleep onstage, the clowns—*BOTTOM,
QUINCE, FLUTE, SNUG, SNOUT, *and* STARVELING—*enter.*

BOTTOM

Are we all here?

QUINCE

Right on time. This is the perfect place to rehearse. This clearing will be the stage, and this hawthorn bush will be our dressing room. Let's put on our play exactly as we'll perform it for the duke.

BOTTOM

Peter Quince—

QUINCE

What is it, jolly Bottom?

BOTTOM

There are things in this comedy of Pyramus and Thisbe that will never work. First of all, Pyramus has to take out a sword to kill himself, which the ladies in the audience won't be able to stand. What should we do about that?

SNOUT

By God, that's a real problem, it's true.

STARVELING

I think we'll have to leave out all the killing, come to think of it.

BOTTOM

Not at all! I've got a plan that will fix everything. Write me a prologue that I can recite to the audience before the play starts. I'll tell them that we won't hurt anyone with our swords, and that Pyramus isn't really dead. And to make it even clearer, we can tell them that I'm playing Pyramus but I'm not really Pyramus—really, I'm Bottom the weaver. That'll keep them from being afraid.

QUINCE

20   Well. We will have such a prologue, and it shall be written
in eight and six.

BOTTOM

No, make it two more. Let it be written in eight and eight.

SNOUT

Will not the ladies be afeard of the lion?

STARVELING

I fear it, I promise you.

BOTTOM

25   Masters, you ought to consider with yourselves. To bring
in—God shield us!—a lion among ladies is a most dreadful
thing. For there is not a more fearful wildfowl than your
lion living. And we ought to look to 't.

SNOUT

Therefore another prologue must tell he is not a lion.

BOTTOM

30   Nay, you must name his name, and half his face must be
seen through the lion's neck. And he himself must speak
through, saying thus—or to the same defect—"Ladies," or
"Fair ladies," "I would wish you" or "I would request you"
or "I would entreat you" "not to fear, not to tremble, my life
35   for yours. If you think I come hither as a lion, it were pity
of my life. No, I am no such thing. I am a man as other men
are." And there indeed let him name his name, and tell
them plainly he is Snug the joiner.

QUINCE

Well, it shall be so. But there is two hard things: that is, to
40   bring the moonlight into a chamber. For, you know,
Pyramus and Thisbe meet by moonlight.

QUINCE

All right, we'll have a prologue then. We'll write it in alternating eight- and six-syllable lines, just like in a ballad.

BOTTOM

No, add a couple more syllables. Make it eight and eight.

SNOUT

Won't the ladies be scared of the lion?

STARVELING

I'm really worried about that.

BOTTOM

Sirs, you ought to think to yourself, bringing in—God forbid!—a lion amongst ladies is really terrible. There's no scarier wild bird than the living lion, and we should remember that.

SNOUT

So we need another prologue to tell everyone he's not a real lion.

BOTTOM

Bottom means to say "something to the same effect."

No, we can just announce the actor's name, and let his face show through the lion costume, and have him say something himself. He should say the following, or something else to the same defect—"Ladies," or "Lovely ladies," "I would like to ask you" or "I would like to request of you" or "I would like to beg you" "not to be afraid, and not to tremble with fear. I value your lives as highly as my own. If you thought I was a real lion, I would be risking my life. But no, I am not at all a lion. I am a man, just like other men." And then he should say his name, and tell them plainly that he's Snug the carpenter.

QUINCE

All right, that's what we'll do then. But there are two things we still have to figure out. How are we going to bring moonlight into a room? Because, you know, Pyramus and Thisbe meet by moonlight.

SNOUT

    Doth the moon shine that night we play our play?

BOTTOM

    A calendar, a calendar! Look in the almanac. Find out
    moonshine, find out moonshine!

QUINCE

45   *(takes out a book)* Yes, it doth shine that night.

BOTTOM

    Why then, may you leave a casement of the great chamber
    window where we play open, and the moon may shine in at
    the casement.

QUINCE

    Ay. Or else one must come in with a bush of thorns and a
50   lantern, and say he comes to disfigure, or to present, the
    person of Moonshine. Then, there is another thing: we
    must have a wall in the great chamber. For Pyramus and
    Thisbe, says the story, did talk through the chink of a wall.

SNOUT

    You can never bring in a wall. What say you, Bottom?

BOTTOM

55   Some man or other must present Wall. And let him have
    some plaster, or some loam, or some roughcast about him
    to signify wall. And let him hold his fingers thus, and
    through that cranny shall Pyramus and Thisbe whisper.

QUINCE

    If that may be then all is well. Come, sit down, every
60   mother's son, and rehearse your parts.—Pyramus, you
    begin. When you have spoken your speech, enter into that
    brake.—And so everyone according to his cue.

SNOUT

Will the moon be shining on the night we're performing our play?

BOTTOM

We need a calendar! Look in the almanac. Look up moonshine, look up moonshine!

QUINCE

(he takes out a book) Yes, the moon will shine that night.

BOTTOM

Well then, you can leave one of the windows open in the big hall where we'll be performing, and the moon can shine in through the window.

QUINCE

Yes, or else someone will have to come in carrying a bundle of sticks and a lantern and say he's come to dis-figure, or represent, the character of Moonshine, because the man in the moon is supposed to carry sticks and a lantern. But there's still another problem: we need to have a wall in the big hall, because according to the story, Pyramus and Thisbe talked through a little hole in a wall.

Bottom means "figure" (symbolize), not "disfigure."

SNOUT

You'll never be able to bring in a wall. What do you think, Bottom?

BOTTOM

Someone should play the part of Wall. He can have some plaster or clay or limestone or something on him to show the audience he's a wall. He can hold his fingers in a V-shape like this, and Pyramus and Thisbe can whisper to each other through that little crack.

QUINCE

If we can do that, everything will be all right. Now sit down, everybody, and rehearse your parts—Pyramus, you start. When you have said your lines, go hide in that bush.—Everyone else, go there too when you're not onstage.

ACT THREE

Enter ROBIN *unseen*

ROBIN
(aside) What hempen homespuns have we swaggering here,
So near the cradle of the fairy queen?

65   What, a play toward? I'll be an auditor.
An actor too, perhaps, if I see cause.

QUINCE
Speak, Pyramus.—Thisbe, stand forth.

BOTTOM
(as PYRAMUS*)* Thisbe, the flowers of odious savors sweet—

QUINCE
"Odors," "odors."

BOTTOM
(as PYRAMUS*)*

                      —odors savors sweet,
So hath thy breath, my dearest Thisbe dear.

70   But hark, a voice! Stay thou but here awhile,
And by and by I will to thee appear.

Exit BOTTOM

ROBIN
(aside) A stranger Pyramus than e'er played here.

Exit ROBIN

FLUTE
Must I speak now?

QUINCE
Ay, marry, must you. For you must understand he goes but

75   to see a noise that he heard, and is to come again.

FLUTE
(as THISBE*)* Most radiant Pyramus, most lily-white of hue,
Of color like the red rose on triumphant brier,
Most brisky juvenal and eke most lovely Jew,
As true as truest horse that yet would never tire.

80   I'll meet thee, Pyramus, at Ninny's tomb.

ROBIN *enters, unseen by the characters onstage.*

ROBIN

> *(to himself)* Who are these country bumpkins swaggering around so close to where the fairy queen is sleeping? What? Are they about to put on a play? I'll watch. And I'll act in it, too, if I feel like it.

QUINCE

> Speak, Pyramus.—Thisbe, come forward.

BOTTOM

> *(as* PYRAMUS*)* Thisbe, flowers with sweet odious smells—

QUINCE

> "Odors," "odors."

BOTTOM

> *(as* PYRAMUS*)* —odors and smells are like your breath, my dearest Thisbe dear. But what's that, a voice! Wait here a while. I'll be right back!
>
> BOTTOM *exits.*

ROBIN

> *(to himself)* That's the strangest Pyramus I've ever seen.
>
> ROBIN *exits.*

FLUTE

> Am I supposed to talk now?

QUINCE

> Yes, you are. You're supposed to show that you understand that Pyramus just went to check on a noise he heard and is coming right back.

FLUTE

> *(as* THISBE*)* Most radiant Pyramus, you are as white as a lily, and the color of a red rose on a splendid rosebush, a very lively young man and also a lovely Jew. You are as reliable as a horse that never gets tired. I'll meet you, Pyramus, at Ninny's grave.

QUINCE

"Ninus' tomb," man. Why, you must not speak that yet.
That you answer to Pyramus. You speak all your part at
once, cues and all.—Pyramus, enter. Your cue is past. It is
"never tire."

FLUTE

85   Oh. *(as* THISBE*)* As true as truest horse that yet would never
tire.

Enter BOTTOM, *with an ass's head, and* ROBIN

BOTTOM

(as PYRAMUS*)* If I were fair, Thisbe, I were only thine.

QUINCE

Oh, monstrous! Oh, strange! We are haunted. Pray,
masters! Fly, masters! Help!

Exeunt QUINCE, FLUTE, SNUG, SNOUT, *and* STARVELING

ROBIN

90   I'll follow you. I'll lead you about a round
Through bog, through bush, through brake, through brier.
Sometime a horse I'll be, sometime a hound,
A hog, a headless bear, sometime a fire.
And neigh, and bark, and grunt, and roar, and burn,
95   Like horse, hound, hog, bear, fire, at every turn.
Exit ROBIN

BOTTOM

Why do they run away? This is a knavery of them to make
me afeard.

Enter SNOUT

QUINCE

That's "Ninus's grave," man. And don't say all of that yet. You're supposed to say some of it as a reply to Pyramus. You just said all your lines at once, cues and all.— Pyramus, enter. You missed your cue. It's "never get tired."

FLUTE

Oh! *(as* THISBE*)* As reliable as a horse that never gets tired.

ROBIN *enters with* BOTTOM, *with a donkey's head instead of a human head.*

BOTTOM

(as PYRAMUS*)* If I were handsome, my lovely Thisbe, I would still want only you.

QUINCE

Help! It's a monster! We're being haunted. Run, everyone, run!

QUINCE, FLUTE, SNUG, SNOUT, *and* STARVELING *exit.*

ROBIN

I'll follow you. I'll run you around in circles, through bogs and bushes and woods and thorns. Sometimes I'll take the shape of a horse, sometimes I'll take the shape of a hound or a pig or a headless bear. Sometimes I'll turn into fire! And I'll neigh like a horse and bark like a hound and grunt like a pig and roar like a bear and burn like a fire at every turn.

ROBIN *exits.*

BOTTOM

Why are they running away? This is some joke of theirs to scare me.

SNOUT *enters.*

ACT THREE

SNOUT

O Bottom, thou art changed! What do I see on thee?

BOTTOM

What do you see? You see an ass head of your own, do you?

Exit SNOUT

Enter QUINCE

QUINCE

00   Bless thee, Bottom, bless thee. Thou art translated.

Exit QUINCE

BOTTOM

I see their knavery: this is to make an ass of me, to fright me if they could. But I will not stir from this place, do what they can. I will walk up and down here and I will sing, that they shall hear I am not afraid.
(sings)

05   *The ouzel cock, so black of hue*
With orange-tawny bill,
The throstle with his note so true,
The wren with little quill—

TITANIA

(waking) What angel wakes me from my flowery bed?

BOTTOM

(sings)

10   *The finch, the sparrow, and the lark,*
The plainsong cuckoo gray,
Whose note full many a man doth mark
And dares not answer "Nay"—

SNOUT

Oh, Bottom, you've changed! What have you got on your head?

BOTTOM

What do you think I've got on my head? You're acting like an ass, don't you think?

SNOUT exits.

QUINCE enters.

QUINCE

God bless you, Bottom, God bless you. You've been changed. Reborn.

QUINCE exits.

BOTTOM

I see what they're up to. They want to make an ass of me, to scare me if they can. But I won't leave this spot, no matter what they do. I'll walk up and down and sing a song, so they'll know I'm not afraid.
(singing)
> The blackbird with its black feathers
> And its orange-and-tan beak,
> The thrush with its clear voice,
> The wren with its small, piping chirp—

TITANIA

(waking up) What angel is this who's waking me up from my bed of flowers?

BOTTOM

(singing)
> The finch, the sparrow, and the lark,
> The gray cuckoo with his simple song
> That many men hear
> But they don't dare say no to it—

For indeed, who would set his wit to so foolish a bird?
115   Who would give a bird the lie, though he cry "cuckoo"
       never so?

TITANIA
       I pray thee, gentle mortal, sing again.
       Mine ear is much enamored of thy note.
       So is mine eye enthrallèd to thy shape.
120   And thy fair virtue's force perforce doth move me
       On the first view to say, to swear, I love thee.

BOTTOM
       Methinks, mistress, you should have little reason for that.
       And yet, to say the truth, reason and love keep little
       company together nowadays. The more the pity that some
125   honest neighbors will not make them friends. Nay, I can
       gleek upon occasion.

TITANIA
       Thou art as wise as thou art beautiful.

BOTTOM
       Not so, neither. But if I had wit enough to get out of this
       wood, I have enough to serve mine own turn.

TITANIA
130   Out of this wood do not desire to go.
       Thou shalt remain here whether thou wilt or no.
       I am a spirit of no common rate.
       The summer still doth tend upon my state.
       And I do love thee. Therefore go with me.
135   I'll give thee fairies to attend on thee.
       And they shall fetch thee jewels from the deep,
       And sing while thou on pressèd flowers dost sleep.
       And I will purge thy mortal grossness so
       That thou shalt like an airy spirit go.—
140   Peaseblossom, Cobweb, Moth, and Mustardseed!

Of course they don't say "no"! Who'd waste his time talking to such a stupid bird? Who'd bother to accuse a bird of lying, even if the bird were telling him that his wife was cheating on him?

Cuckoos symbolize cuckolds (men whose wives cheat on them). The cuckoo's song was sometimes imagined as a mocking accusation that the men who hear it are cuckolds.

TITANIA

Please sing again, sweet human. I love to listen to your voice, and I love to look at your body. I know this is the first time I've ever seen you, but you're so wonderful that I can't help swearing to you that I love you.

BOTTOM

I don't think you've got much of a reason to love me. But to tell you the truth, reason and love have very little to do with each other these days. It's too bad some mutual friend of theirs doesn't introduce them. Ha, ha! No, I'm just kidding.

TITANIA

You're as wise as you are beautiful.

BOTTOM

No, that's not true. But if I were smart enough to get out of this forest, I'd be wise enough to satisfy myself.

TITANIA

Don't bother wishing you could leave this forest, because you're going to stay here whether you want to or not. I'm no ordinary fairy. I rule over the summer, and I love you. So come with me. I'll give you fairies as servants, and they'll bring you jewels from the depths of the ocean, and sing to you while you sleep on a bed of flowers. And I'll turn you into a spirit like us, so you won't die as humans do.—Come here, Peaseblossom, Cobweb, Moth, and Mustardseed!

ACT THREE

Enter four fairies: PEASEBLOSSOM, COBWEB, MOTH, *and*
MUSTARDSEED

PEASEBLOSSOM
Ready.

COBWEB
                And I.

MOTH
                        And I.

MUSTARDSEED
                                And I.

ALL
        Where shall we go?

TITANIA
        Be kind and courteous to this gentleman.
        Hop in his walks and gambol in his eyes.
145   Feed him with apricoks and dewberries,
        With purple grapes, green figs, and mulberries.
        The honey bags steal from the humble-bees,
        And for night tapers crop their waxen thighs
        And light them at the fiery glowworms' eyes
150   To have my love to bed and to arise.
        And pluck the wings from painted butterflies
        To fan the moonbeams from his sleeping eyes.
        Nod to him, elves, and do him courtesies.

PEASEBLOSSOM
        Hail, mortal.

COBWEB
                Hail.

MOTH
                        Hail.

MUSTARDSEED
                                Hail.

BOTTOM
155   I cry your worships' mercy, heartily.—I beseech your
        worship's name.

Four fairies—PEASEBLOSSOM, COBWEB, MOTH, *and* MUSTARDSEED—*enter.*

PEASEBLOSSOM
Ready.

COBWEB
Me too.

MOTH
Me too.

MUSTARDSEED
And me too.

ALL
Where should we go?

TITANIA
Be kind and polite to this gentleman. Follow him around. Leap and dance for him. Feed him apricots and blackberries, with purple grapes, green figs, and mulberries. Steal honey from the bumblebees, and make candles out of the bees' wax. Light them with the light of glowworms, so my love will have light when he goes to bed and wakes up. Pluck off colorful butterfly wings, and use them to fan moonbeams away from his eyes as he sleeps. Bow to him, fairies, and curtsy to him.

PEASEBLOSSOM
Hello, mortal!

COBWEB
Hello!

MOTH
Hello!

MUSTARDSEED
Hello!

BOTTOM
I beg your pardon, sirs.—Please tell me your name, sir?

ACT THREE

COBWEB
Cobweb.

BOTTOM
I shall desire you of more acquaintance, good Master
Cobweb. If I cut my finger, I shall make bold with you.—
160 Your name, honest gentleman?

PEASEBLOSSOM
Peaseblossom.

BOTTOM
I pray you, commend me to Mistress Squash, your mother,
and to Master Peascod, your father. Good Master
Peaseblossom, I shall desire you of more acquaintance
165 too.— Your name, I beseech you, sir?

MUSTARDSEED
Mustardseed.

BOTTOM
Good Master Mustardseed, I know your patience well.
That same cowardly, giantlike ox-beef hath devoured
many a gentleman of your house. I promise you your
170 kindred hath made my eyes water ere now. I desire you of
more acquaintance, good Master Mustardseed.

TITANIA
Come, wait upon him. Lead him to my bower.
The moon methinks looks with a watery eye.
And when she weeps, weeps every little flower,
175 Lamenting some enforcèd chastity.
Tie up my love's tongue. Bring him silently.

Exeunt

COBWEB

Cobweb.

BOTTOM

I'd like to get to know you better, Mr. Cobweb. If I cut my finger, I'll use you as a bandage to stop the bleeding.—And your name, sir?

PEASEBLOSSOM

Peaseblossom.

BOTTOM

Please, give my regards to your mother, Mrs. Peapod, and your father, Mr. Peapod. Good Mr. Peaseblossom, I'd like to get to know you better too.—And you, may I ask what your name is, sir?

MUSTARDSEED

Mustardseed.

BOTTOM

Good Mr. Mustardseed, I know you very well. Those cowardly, gigantic sides of beef have been responsible for many of your family members getting eaten as a condiment on beef. I swear to you, many members of your mustard family have made my eyes water before. I look forward to getting to know you better, Mr. Mustardseed.

TITANIA

Take good care of him. Take him to my sleeping area. The moon looks sad to me. When she cries, all the little flowers cry too. They're sad because someone is prevented from having sex—or is having it against her will. Keep my lover quiet. Bring him to me in silence.

They all exit.

ACT THREE, Scene 2

Enter OBERON, *King of Fairies, solus*

OBERON
    I wonder if Titania be awaked.
    Then, what it was that next came in her eye,
    Which she must dote on in extremity.

Enter ROBIN

    Here comes my messenger.—How now, mad spirit?
5   What night-rule now about this haunted grove?

ROBIN
    My mistress with a monster is in love.
    Near to her close and consecrated bower,
    While she was in her dull and sleeping hour,
    A crew of patches, rude mechanicals
10   That work for bread upon Athenian stalls,
    Were met together to rehearse a play
    Intended for great Theseus' nuptial day.
    The shallowest thick-skin of that barren sort,
    Who Pyramus presented in their sport,
15   Forsook his scene and entered in a brake,
    When I did him at this advantage take,
    An ass's nole I fixèd on his head.
    Anon his Thisbe must be answerèd,
    And forth my mimic comes. When they him spy,
20   As wild geese that the creeping fowler eye,
    Or russet-pated choughs, many in sort,
    Rising and cawing at the gun's report,
    Sever themselves and madly sweep the sky—
    So at his sight away his fellows fly;
25   And, at our stamp, here o'er and o'er one falls.

ACT THREE, Scene 2

OBERON, *the Fairy King, enters.*

OBERON

I wonder if Titania is awake yet, and if she is, I wonder what the first thing she saw was. Whatever it is, she must be completely in love with it now.

ROBIN *enters.*

Ah, here comes my messenger.—What's going on, you crazy spirit? What havoc have you wreaked in this part of the forest?

ROBIN

My mistress Titania is in love with a monster. While she was sleeping in her bed of flowers, a group of bumbling idiots, rough workmen from Athens, got together nearby to rehearse some play they plan to perform on Theseus's wedding day. The stupidest one, who played Pyramus in their play, finished his scene and went to sit in the bushes to wait for his next cue. I took that opportunity to stick a donkey's head on him. When it was time for him to go back onstage and talk to his Thisbe, he came out of the bushes and everyone saw him. His friends ran away as fast as ducks scatter when they hear a hunter's gunshot. One of them was so frightened when he heard my footsteps that he yelled, "Murder!" and called for help from Athens. They were all so afraid that they completely lost their common sense. They started to become scared of inanimate objects, terrified by the thorns and briars that catch at their clothing and pull off their sleeves and hats. I led them on in this frightened, dis-

He "Murder!" cries and help from Athens calls.
Their sense thus weak, lost with their fears thus strong,
Made senseless things begin to do them wrong.
For briers and thorns at their apparel snatch,
30   Some sleeves, some hats—from yielders all things catch.
I led them on in this distracted fear
And left sweet Pyramus translated there.
When in that moment so it came to pass,
Titania waked and straightway loved an ass.

OBERON
35   This falls out better than I could devise.
But hast thou yet latched the Athenian's eyes
With the love juice, as I did bid thee do?

ROBIN
I took him sleeping—that is finished too—
And the Athenian woman by his side,
40   That, when he waked, of force she must be eyed.

Enter DEMETRIUS *and* HERMIA

OBERON
(aside to ROBIN*)* Stand close. This is the same Athenian.

ROBIN
(aside to OBERON*)* This is the woman, but not this the man.

DEMETRIUS
Oh, why rebuke you him that loves you so?
Lay breath so bitter on your bitter foe.

HERMIA
45   Now I but chide, but I should use thee worse.
For thou, I fear, hast given me cause to curse.
If thou hast slain Lysander in his sleep,
Being o'er shoes in blood, plunge in the deep,
And kill me too.

tracted state, and left sweet Pyramus there, transformed into someone with a donkey's head. At that exact moment, Titania woke up and immediately fell in love with him, an ass.

OBERON

This is going even better than I planned. But have you put the love juice from the flower on the eyes of that Athenian, as I asked you to do?

ROBIN

Yes, I found him when he was asleep—so that's taken care of too—and the Athenian woman was sleeping near him. When he woke up, he must have seen her.

DEMETRIUS *and* HERMIA *enter.*

OBERON

(speaking so that only ROBIN *can hear)* Step aside. Here's the Athenian coming now.

ROBIN

(speaking so that only OBERON *can hear)* That's definitely the woman I saw, but it's not the same man.

DEMETRIUS

Why are you so rude to someone who loves you so much? Save that kind of harsh language for your worst enemy.

HERMIA

I'm only scolding you now, but I should treat you much worse, because I'm afraid you've given me good reason to curse you. If you killed Lysander while he was sleeping, then you're already up to your ankles in blood. You might as well jump right into a bloodbath

50 The sun was not so true unto the day
As he to me. Would he have stolen away
From sleeping Hermia? I'll believe as soon
This whole Earth may be bored, and that the moon
May through the center creep and so displease
55 Her brother's noontide with th' Antipodes.
It cannot be but thou hast murdered him.
So should a murderer look, so dead, so grim.

DEMETRIUS
So should the murdered look, and so should I,
Pierced through the heart with your stern cruelty.
60 Yet you, the murderer, look as bright, as clear,
As yonder Venus in her glimmering sphere.

HERMIA
What's this to my Lysander? Where is he?
Ah, good Demetrius, wilt thou give him me?

DEMETRIUS
I had rather give his carcass to my hounds.

HERMIA
65 Out, dog! Out, cur! Thou drivest me past the bounds
Of maiden's patience. Hast thou slain him then?
Henceforth be never numbered among men!
Oh, once tell true, tell true even for my sake—
Durst thou have looked upon him being awake,
70 And hast thou killed him sleeping? O brave touch!
Could not a worm, an adder, do so much?
An adder did it, for with doubler tongue
Than thine, thou serpent, never adder stung.

DEMETRIUS
You spend your passion on a misprised mood.
75 I am not guilty of Lysander's blood.
Nor is he dead, for aught that I can tell.

HERMIA
I pray thee, tell me then that he is well.

DEMETRIUS
An if I could, what should I get therefore?

and kill me, too. He was more faithful to me than the sun is to the daytime. Would he have snuck away from me while I was asleep? I'll believe that when I believe that there's a hole through the center of the earth, and the moon has passed all the way through to the other side. The only possibility is that you've murdered him. A murderer should look like you do, so pale and grim.

DEMETRIUS

That's how someone who's been murdered should look, and that's how I look. You've pierced me through the heart with your cruelty, and yet you, the murderer, look as bright and clear as a star in the sky.

HERMIA

What does that have to do with my Lysander? Where is he? Oh, good Demetrius, will you find him for me?

DEMETRIUS

I would rather feed his corpse to my dogs.

HERMIA

Get out, dog! You've driven me to my wit's end. Did you kill him, then? From now on I won't even consider you a human being. Oh, just tell the truth for once. tell the truth, if only for my sake.—Would you have even dared to look at him when he was awake? And did you kill him while he was sleeping? Oh, how brave of you! A snake could do that as easily as you could. A snake did do it, because no snake ever had a more forked, lying tongue than you have.

DEMETRIUS

You're getting all worked up over a misunderstanding. I didn't kill Lysander. As far as I know, he's not even dead.

HERMIA

Then please tell me he's all right.

DEMETRIUS

If I told you that, what would I get out of it?

HERMIA
A privilege never to see me more.
80   And from thy hated presence part I so.
See me no more, whether he be dead or no.

Exit HERMIA

DEMETRIUS
There is no following her in this fierce vein.
Here therefore for a while I will remain.
So sorrow's heaviness doth heavier grow
85   For debt that bankrupt sleep doth sorrow owe,
Which now in some slight measure it will pay,
If for his tender here I make some stay.
(lies down and sleeps)

OBERON
(to ROBIN*)* What hast thou done? Thou hast mistaken quite,
And laid the love juice on some true love's sight.
90   Of thy misprision must perforce ensue
Some true love turned, and not a false turned true.

ROBIN
Then fate o'errules that, one man holding troth,
A million fail, confounding oath on oath.

OBERON
About the wood go swifter than the wind,
95   And Helena of Athens look thou find—
All fancy-sick she is and pale of cheer,
With sighs of love, that costs the fresh blood dear.
By some illusion see thou bring her here.
I'll charm his eyes against she do appear.

ROBIN
100   I go, I go. Look how I go,
Swifter than arrow from the Tartar's bow.

Exit ROBIN

HERMIA

The privilege of never seeing me again. And now I'm going to leave your despised company. You'll never see me again, whether or not he's dead.

HERMIA *exits.*

DEMETRIUS

I can't go after her when she's in a rage like this. So I'll stay here for a while. Sadness gets worse when you haven't had enough sleep. I'll try to sleep a little here. (DEMETRIUS *lies down and falls asleep)*

OBERON

(to ROBIN*)* What have you done? You've made a mistake and put the love-juice on someone else, someone who was truly in love. Because of your mistake someone's true love must have turned bad, instead of this man's false love being turned into a true love.

ROBIN

In that case, it must be fate. That's the way of the world. For every man who's faithful to his true love, a million end up running after a different lover.

OBERON

Go around the forest, moving faster than the wind, and make sure you find Helena of Athens.—She's lovesick, and her face is pale from all the sighing she's been doing, because sighing is bad for the blood. Bring her here with some trick or illusion, and I'll put the charm on his eyes for when she comes.

ROBIN

I go, I go, look at me go—faster than an arrow from a Tartar's bow.

The Tartars were a people from Asia Minor famous for their archery.

ROBIN *exits*

OBERON
(squeezing flower juice into DEMETRIUS*'s eyes)*
Flower of this purple dye,
Hit with Cupid's archery,
Sink in apple of his eye.
105   When his love he doth espy,
Let her shine as gloriously
As the Venus of the sky.
When thou wakest, if she be by,
Beg of her for remedy.

Enter ROBIN

ROBIN
110   Captain of our fairy band,
Helena is here at hand,
And the youth, mistook by me,
Pleading for a lover's fee.
Shall we their fond pageant see?
115   Lord, what fools these mortals be!

OBERON
Stand aside. The noise they make
Will cause Demetrius to awake.

ROBIN
Then will two at once woo one.
That must needs be sport alone.
120   And those things do best please me
That befall preposterously.

Enter LYSANDER *and* HELENA

LYSANDER
Why should you think that I should woo in scorn?
Scorn and derision never come in tears.
Look, when I vow, I weep. And vows so born,
125   In their nativity all truth appears.

OBERON

(putting flower juice on DEMETRIUS*'s eyelids)*
You purple flower, hit by Cupid's arrow, sink into the pupils of this man's eyes. When he sees the girl he should love, make her seem as bright to him as the evening star. Young man, when you wake up, if she's nearby, beg her to cure your lovesickness.

ROBIN *enters.*

ROBIN

Helena is nearby, boss. The young man who I mistook for this one is there too, begging her to love him. Should we watch this ridiculous scene? Lord, what fools these mortals are!

OBERON

Step aside. The noise they're making will wake up Demetrius.

ROBIN

Then the two of them will both pursue one girl. That will be funny enough, and preposterous situations are my favorite thing.

LYSANDER *and* HELENA *enter.*

LYSANDER

Why do you think I'm making fun of you when I tell you I love you? People don't cry when they're mocking someone. Look, when I swear that I love you, I cry, and when someone cries while he's making a promise, he's

How can these things in me seem scorn to you,
Bearing the badge of faith to prove them true?

HELENA
You do advance your cunning more and more.
When truth kills truth, O devilish holy fray!
130   These vows are Hermia's. Will you give her o'er?
Weigh oath with oath, and you will nothing weigh.
Your vows to her and me, put in two scales,
Will even weigh, and both as light as tales.

LYSANDER
I had no judgment when to her I swore.

HELENA
135   Nor none, in my mind, now you give her o'er.

LYSANDER
Demetrius loves her, and he loves not you.

DEMETRIUS
(waking) O Helena, goddess, nymph, perfect, divine!
To what, my love, shall I compare thine eyne?
Crystal is muddy. Oh, how ripe in show
140   Thy lips, those kissing cherries, tempting grow!
That pure congealèd white, high Taurus' snow,
Fanned with the eastern wind, turns to a crow
When thou hold'st up thy hand. Oh, let me kiss
This princess of pure white, this seal of bliss!

HELENA
145   O spite! O hell! I see you all are bent
To set against me for your merriment.
If you were civil and knew courtesy,
You would not do me thus much injury.
Can you not hate me, as I know you do,
150   But you must join in souls to mock me too?
If you were men, as men you are in show,
You would not use a gentle lady so

usually telling the truth. How can it seem like I'm making fun of you, when my tears prove that I'm sincere?

HELENA

You get trickier and trickier. You've made the same promises to me and to Hermia—they can't both be true! They must both be false. The promises you're making to me belong to Hermia. Will you abandon her? If you weighed the promises you made to me against the promises you made to her, they'd come out the same—they both weigh nothing. They're lies.

LYSANDER

I wasn't thinking clearly when I made those promises to her.

HELENA

And I don't believe you're thinking clearly now, as you break those promises.

LYSANDER

Demetrius loves her, and he doesn't love you.

DEMETRIUS

(waking up) Oh Helena, you goddess, you divine and perfect nymph! What can I compare your eyes to? Crystal isn't as clear as they are. Oh, your lips are as ripe as a pair of tempting cherries touching each other! The pure white of the snow on a mountaintop seems black as a crow's wing next to the whiteness of your hands. Oh, let me kiss your beautiful white hand. It'll make me so happy!

HELENA

Damn it! I see you're all determined to gang up on me for a few laughs. If you had any manners at all, you wouldn't treat me like this. Can't you just hate me, as I know you do? Do you have to get together to humiliate me too? If you were real men, as you pretend to be, you wouldn't treat a lady this way, making vows and promises and praising my beauty when I know you're really both disgusted by me. You're competing for

To vow, and swear, and superpraise my parts,
When I am sure you hate me with your hearts.
155   You both are rivals, and love Hermia,
And now both rivals to mock Helena—
A trim exploit, a manly enterprise,
To conjure tears up in a poor maid's eyes
With your derision! None of noble sort
160   Would so offend a virgin, and extort
A poor soul's patience, all to make you sport.

LYSANDER
You are unkind, Demetrius. Be not so.
For you love Hermia. This you know I know.
And here, with all good will, with all my heart,
165   In Hermia's love I yield you up my part.
And yours of Helena to me bequeath,
Whom I do love and will do till my death.

HELENA
Never did mockers waste more idle breath.

DEMETRIUS
Lysander, keep thy Hermia. I will none.
170   If e'er I loved her, all that love is gone.
My heart to her but as guest-wise sojourned,
And now to Helen is it home returned,
There to remain.

LYSANDER
Helen, it is not so.

DEMETRIUS
175   Disparage not the faith thou dost not know,
Lest to thy peril thou aby it dear.
Look, where thy love comes. Yonder is thy dear.

Enter HERMIA

HERMIA
Dark night, that from the eye his function takes,
The ear more quick of apprehension makes.

Hermia's love, and now you're competing to see which one of you can make fun of me the most. That's a great idea, a really manly thing to do—making a poor girl cry! No respectable person would offend an innocent girl just to have some fun.

LYSANDER

Don't be cruel, Demetrius. I know you love Hermia, and you know I know it. Right here, right now, I swear I'm giving up all my claims on her and handing her to you. In exchange, give up your claim to love Helena, since I love her and will love her until I die.

HELENA

Nobody's ever gone to so much trouble just to make fun of someone.

DEMETRIUS

Lysander, keep your Hermia. I don't want her. If I ever loved her, all that love is gone now. My love for her was temporary. Now I'll love Helena forever.

LYSANDER

Helena, it's not true.

DEMETRIUS

Don't insult a deep love that you don't understand, or you'll pay the price. Look, here comes the woman you love.

HERMIA *enters.*

HERMIA

It's hard to see clearly in the dark of night, but it's easier to hear well. I couldn't see you, Lysander, but I

ACT THREE

180   Wherein it doth impair the seeing sense,
It pays the hearing double recompense.
Thou art not by mine eye, Lysander, found.
Mine ear, I thank it, brought me to thy sound
But why unkindly didst thou leave me so?

LYSANDER
185   Why should he stay, whom love doth press to go?

HERMIA
What love could press Lysander from my side?

LYSANDER
Lysander's love, that would not let him bide,
Fair Helena, who more engilds the night
Than all yon fiery oes and eyes of light.
190   Why seek'st thou me? Could not this make thee know
The hate I bear thee made me leave thee so?

HERMIA
You speak not as you think. It cannot be.

HELENA
Lo, she is one of this confederacy!
Now I perceive they have conjoined all three
195   To fashion this false sport, in spite of me.—
Injurious Hermia! Most ungrateful maid!
Have you conspired, have you with these contrived
To bait me with this foul derision?
Is all the counsel that we two have shared,
200   The sisters' vows, the hours that we have spent
When we have chid the hasty-footed time
For parting us—oh, is it all forgot?
All schooldays' friendship, childhood innocence?
We, Hermia, like two artificial gods,
205   Have with our needles created both one flower,
Both on one sampler, sitting on one cushion,
Both warbling of one song, both in one key,
As if our hands, our sides, voices, and minds,
Had been incorporate. So we grew together,
210   Like to a double cherry—seeming parted

heard your voice, and that's how I found you. Why did you leave me alone so unkindly?

LYSANDER

Why stay when love tells you to go?

HERMIA

But what love could make my Lysander leave me?

LYSANDER

I had to hurry to my love, beautiful Helena, who lights up the night better than all those fiery stars. Why are you looking for me? Didn't you figure out that I left you because I hate you?

HERMIA

You can't mean what you're saying. It's impossible.

HELENA

So, she's in on this too! Now I see that all three of them have gotten together to play this cruel trick on me. Hurtful Hermia, you ungrateful girl, have you conspired with these two to provoke me with this horrible teasing? Have you forgotten all the talks we've had together, the vows we made to be like sisters to one another, all the hours we spent together, wishing that we never had to say goodbye—have you forgotten? Our friendship in our schooldays, our childhood innocence? We used to sit together and sew one flower with our two needles, sewing it on one piece of cloth, sitting on the same cushion, singing one song in the same key, as if our hands, our sides, our voices and our minds were stuck together. We grew together like twin cherries—which seemed to be separate but were also together—two lovely cherries on one stem. We seemed to have two separate bodies, but we had one heart. Do you want to destroy our old friendship by

But yet an union in partition—
Two lovely berries molded on one stem;
So, with two seeming bodies but one heart,
Two of the first, like coats in heraldry,
215 Due but to one and crownèd with one crest.
And will you rent our ancient love asunder
To join with men in scorning your poor friend?
It is not friendly, 'tis not maidenly.
Our sex, as well as I, may chide you for it,
220 Though I alone do feel the injury.

HERMIA
I am amazèd at your passionate words.
I scorn you not. It seems that you scorn me.

HELENA
Have you not set Lysander, as in scorn,
To follow me and praise my eyes and face?
225 And made your other love, Demetrius—
Who even but now did spurn me with his foot—
To call me goddess, nymph, divine, and rare,
Precious, celestial? Wherefore speaks he this
To her he hates? And wherefore doth Lysander
230 Deny your love, so rich within his soul,
And tender me, forsooth, affection,
But by your setting on, by your consent?
What though I be not so in grace as you—
So hung upon with love, so fortunate—
235 But miserable most, to love unloved?
This you should pity rather than despise.

HERMIA
I understand not what you mean by this.

HELENA
Ay, do. Persever, counterfeit sad looks,
Make mouths upon me when I turn my back,
240 Wink each at other, hold the sweet jest up—
This sport, well carried, shall be chronicled.
If you have any pity, grace, or manners,

joining these men to insult your poor friend? It's not friendly, and it's not ladylike. All women would be angry with you for doing it, even though I'm the only one who's hurt by it.

HERMIA

I'm completely dumbfounded by what you're saying. I'm not insulting you. It sounds more like you're insulting me.

HELENA

Come on, confess. Didn't you send Lysander, as an insult, to follow me around praising my eyes and my face? Haven't you made your other love, Demetrius—who kicked me with his foot not long ago—call me a goddess and a divine, rare, precious, heavenly creature? Why does he talk like that to a girl he can't stand? And why does Lysander deny that he loves you, when he loves you so deeply? Why would he show me any affection, unless you told him to? Why does it matter that I'm not as lucky or lovable as you are and that the love I feel is unrequited? You should pity me for that reason, not hate me.

HERMIA

I don't know what you're talking about.

HELENA

Oh, fine. All right, go ahead, keep up your little game, pretend to be sympathetic, but then nudge each other and wink and make faces at me when I turn my back. Keep up your wonderful game. You're doing such a good job on this trick, someone should write a book

You would not make me such an argument.
But fare ye well. 'Tis partly my own fault,
245   Which death or absence soon shall remedy.

LYSANDER
Stay, gentle Helena. Hear my excuse.
My love, my life, my soul, fair Helena!

HELENA
Oh, excellent!

HERMIA
(to LYSANDER*)*
                              Sweet, do not scorn her so.

DEMETRIUS
If she cannot entreat, I can compel.

LYSANDER
Thou canst compel no more than she entreat.
250   Thy threats have no more strength than her weak prayers.—
Helen, I love thee. By my life, I do.
I swear by that which I will lose for thee
To prove him false that says I love thee not.

DEMETRIUS
I say I love thee more than he can do.

LYSANDER
255   If thou say so, withdraw and prove it too.

DEMETRIUS
Quick, come.

HERMIA
                              Lysander, whereto tends all this?
(holds LYSANDER *back)*

LYSANDER
(to HERMIA*)*   Away, you Ethiope!

DEMETRIUS
(to HERMIA*)*
                              No, no. He'll

about it. If you had any sense of pity, or manners, you wouldn't pretend to fight over me like this. But goodbye. It's partly my own fault, since I followed you here. Leaving—or dying—will soon take care of everything.

LYSANDER

Stay, lovely Helena. Listen to my excuse. My love, my life, my soul, beautiful Helena!

HELENA

That's a good one.

HERMIA

(to LYSANDER*)* Don't insult her like that, Lysander darling.

DEMETRIUS

(to LYSANDER*)* If Hermia's begging can't make you stop insulting Helena, I can force you to do so.

LYSANDER

You can't force me any more than Hermia can beg me. Your threats are no stronger than her whining.—Helena, I love you. I swear I do. I'll give my life for you, just to prove this guy wrong when he says I don't love you.

DEMETRIUS

I say that I love you more than he does.

LYSANDER

If that's what you say, go fight a duel with me and prove it.

DEMETRIUS

You're on. Let's do it.

HERMIA

Lysander, where are you going with all this?
(she holds LYSANDER *back)*

LYSANDER

(to HERMIA*)* Get away, you African!

DEMETRIUS

(to HERMIA*)* No, no. He'll act like he's going to break

Seem to break loose.
(*to* LYSANDER)
                              Take on as you would follow,
But yet come not. You are a tame man, go!

LYSANDER
(*to* HERMIA) Hang off, thou cat, thou burr! Vile thing, let loose
260   Or I will shake thee from me like a serpent.

HERMIA
Why are you grown so rude? What change is this,
Sweet love?

LYSANDER
                              Thy love? Out, tawny Tartar, out!
Out, loathèd medicine! O hated potion, hence!

HERMIA
Do you not jest?

HELENA
                              Yes, sooth, and so do you.

LYSANDER
265   Demetrius, I will keep my word with thee.

DEMETRIUS
I would I had your bond, for I perceive
A weak bond holds you. I'll not trust your word.

LYSANDER
What, should I hurt her, strike her, kill her dead?
Although I hate her, I'll not harm her so.

HERMIA
(*to* LYSANDER)
270   What, can you do me greater harm than hate?
Hate me? Wherefore? O me! What news, my love?
Am not I Hermia? Are not you Lysander?
I am as fair now as I was erewhile.
Since night you loved me. Yet since night you left me.
275   Why then, you left me—Oh, the gods forbid!—
In earnest, shall I say?

LYSANDER
                              Ay, by my life,

free from you, Hermia. *(to* LYSANDER*)* Pretend like you're going to follow me, but then don't come. You're a coward, get out of here!

LYSANDER

(to HERMIA*)* Stop hanging on me, you cat, you thorn. Let go of me, or I'll shake you off like a snake.

HERMIA

Why have you gotten so rude? What's happened to you, my darling?

LYSANDER

Your darling? Get out, you dark-skinned gypsy! Get out, you horrible poison. Get out!

HERMIA

Are you joking?

HELENA

Of course he is, and so are you.

LYSANDER

Demetrius, I'm ready to fight you as promised.

DEMETRIUS

I wish we had a signed legal contract. I can see you don't keep your promises very well. I don't trust you.

LYSANDER

What? Do you want me to hit Hermia, hurt her, kill her? Sure, I hate her, but I wouldn't hurt her.

HERMIA

(to LYSANDER*)* Can you hurt me any more than by saying you hate me? Hate me? Why? What's happened to you, my love? Am I not Hermia? Aren't you Lysander? I'm as beautiful now as I was a little while ago. You still loved me when we fell asleep, but when you woke up you left me. So you left me—Oh, God help me!—For real?

LYSANDER

I certainly did, and I never wanted to see you again. So stop hoping and wondering what I mean. I've spelled

And never did desire to see thee more.
Therefore be out of hope, of question, of doubt.
Be certain, nothing truer. 'Tis no jest
280   That I do hate thee and love Helena.

HERMIA
O me!
(to HELENA*)* You juggler! You canker-blossom!
You thief of love! What, have you come by night
And stol'n my love's heart from him?

HELENA
                              Fine, i' faith!
285   Have you no modesty, no maiden shame,
No touch of bashfulness? What, will you tear
Impatient answers from my gentle tongue?
Fie, fie! You counterfeit, you puppet, you!

HERMIA
"Puppet"? Why so?—Ay, that way goes the game.
290   Now I perceive that she hath made compare
Between our statures. She hath urged her height,
And with her personage, her tall personage,
Her height, forsooth, she hath prevailed with him.—
And are you grown so high in his esteem
295   Because I am so dwarfish and so low?
How low am I, thou painted maypole? Speak.
How low am I? I am not yet so low
But that my nails can reach unto thine eyes.

HELENA
(to LYSANDER *and* DEMETRIUS*)*
I pray you, though you mock me, gentlemen,
300   Let her not hurt me. I was never cursed.
I have no gift at all in shrewishness.
I am a right maid for my cowardice.
Let her not strike me. You perhaps may think,
Because she is something lower than myself,
305   That I can match her.

it out for you clearly. It's no joke. I hate you and love Helena.

HERMIA

Oh, no! *(to* HELENA*)* You trickster, you snake! You thief! What, did you sneak in at night and steal my love's heart from him?

HELENA

Oh, that's very nice! You ought to be ashamed of yourself! You're going to make me mad enough to answer you? Damn you, you faker, you puppet!

HERMIA

"Puppet"? Why "puppet"?—Oh, I see where this is going. She's talking about our difference in height. She's paraded in front of him to show off how tall she is. She won him over with her height.—Does he have such a high opinion of you because I'm so short? Is that it? So how short am I, you painted barber pole? Tell me. How short am I? I'm not too short to gouge your eyes out with my fingernails.

HELENA

(to LYSANDER *and* DEMETRIUS*)* Please don't let her hurt me, gentlemen, however much you want to tease me. I never was much good with insults. I'm not mean and catty like her. I'm a nice shy girl. Please don't let her hit me. Maybe you think that because she's shorter than me I can take her.

HERMIA

                          "Lower"? Hark, again!

HELENA

Good Hermia, do not be so bitter with me.
I evermore did love you, Hermia,
Did ever keep your counsels, never wronged you—
Save that, in love unto Demetrius,

310   I told him of your stealth unto this wood.
He followed you. For love I followed him.
But he hath chid me hence and threatened me
To strike me, spurn me—nay, to kill me too.
And now, so you will let me quiet go,

315   To Athens will I bear my folly back
And follow you no further. Let me go.
You see how simple and how fond I am.

HERMIA

Why, get you gone! Who is 't that hinders you?

HELENA

A foolish heart, that I leave here behind.

HERMIA

320   What, with Lysander?

HELENA

                     With Demetrius.

LYSANDER

Be not afraid. She shall not harm thee, Helena.

DEMETRIUS

(to LYSANDER*)*
No, sir, she shall not, though you take her part.

HELENA

Oh, when she's angry, she is keen and shrewd!
She was a vixen when she went to school.

325   And though she be but little, she is fierce.

HERMIA

"Little" again? Nothing but "low" and "little"!—
Why will you suffer her to flout me thus?
Let me come to her.

HERMIA

"Shorter!" See, she's doing it again!

HELENA

Good Hermia, please don't act so bitter toward me. I always loved you, Hermia, and gave you advice. I never did anything to hurt you—except once, when I told Demetrius that you planned to sneak off into this forest. And I only did that because I loved Demetrius so much. He followed you. And I followed him because I loved him. But he told me to get lost and threatened to hit me, kick me—even kill me. Now just let me go quietly back to Athens. I'll carry my mistakes back with me. I won't follow you anymore. Please let me go. You see how naïve and foolish I've been.

HERMIA

Well, get out of here then! What's keeping you?

HELENA

My stupid heart, which I'm leaving behind here.

HERMIA

What, you're leaving it with Lysander?

HELENA

No, with Demetrius.

LYSANDER

Don't be afraid. She can't hurt you, Helena.

DEMETRIUS

(to LYSANDER*)* That's right, Hermia won't hurt Helena even if you try to help her.

HELENA

Oh, when you get her angry, she's a good fighter, and vicious too. She was a hellcat in school. And she's fierce, even though she's little.

HERMIA

"Little" again? Nothing but "little" and "short"!— Why are you letting her insult me like this? Let me at her!.

LYSANDER
(to HERMIA)   Get you gone, you dwarf,
You minimus of hindering knotgrass made,
330   You bead, you acorn!

DEMETRIUS
                          You are too officious
In her behalf that scorns your services.
Let her alone. Speak not of Helena.
Take not her part. For if thou dost intend
Never so little show of love to her,
335   Thou shalt aby it.

LYSANDER
                          Now she holds me not.
Now follow, if thou darest, to try whose right,
Of thine or mine, is most in Helena.

DEMETRIUS
"Follow"? Nay, I'll go with thee, cheek by jowl.

Exeunt LYSANDER *and* DEMETRIUS

HERMIA
You, mistress, all this coil is long of you.
340   Nay, go not back.

HELENA
                    I will not trust you, I,
Nor longer stay in your curst company.
Your hands than mine are quicker for a fray.
My legs are longer though, to run away.

Exit HELENA

HERMIA
I am amazed and know not what to say.

Exit HERMIA

OBERON
345   (to ROBIN) This is thy negligence. Still thou mistakest,
Or else committ'st thy knaveries willfully.

LYSANDER

(to HERMIA*)* Get lost, you dwarf, you tiny little weed, you scrap, you acorn!

DEMETRIUS

You're doing too much to defend a woman who wants nothing to do with you. Leave Hermia alone. Don't talk about Helena. Don't take Helena's side. If you continue treating Hermia so badly, you'll pay for it.

LYSANDER

Hermia's not holding onto me anymore. Follow me if you're brave enough, and we'll fight over Helena.

DEMETRIUS

"Follow"? No, I'll walk right next to you, side by side.

DEMETRIUS *and* LYSANDER *exit.*

HERMIA

All this fighting is because of you. Stay where you are.

HELENA

I'm not sticking around here any more. I don't trust you. You might be a better fighter than I am, but my legs are longer and I can run away faster.

HELENA *exits.*

HERMIA

I just can't believe any of this. I don't know what to say.

HERMIA *exits.*

OBERON

(to ROBIN*)* This is all your fault. You make mistakes constantly, or else you cause this kind of trouble on purpose.

ROBIN

Believe me, King of Shadows, I mistook.
Did not you tell me I should know the man
By the Athenian garment he had on?
350 And so far blameless proves my enterprise,
That I have 'nointed an Athenian's eyes.
And so far am I glad it so did sort,
As this their jangling I esteem a sport.

OBERON

Thou seest these lovers seek a place to fight.
355 Hie therefore, Robin, overcast the night.
The starry welkin cover thou anon
With drooping fog as black as Acheron,
And lead these testy rivals so astray
As one come not within another's way.
360 Like to Lysander sometime frame thy tongue,
Then stir Demetrius up with bitter wrong.
And sometime rail thou like Demetrius.
And from each other look thou lead them thus,
Till o'er their brows death-counterfeiting sleep
365 With leaden legs and batty wings doth creep.
(gives ROBIN *another flower)*
Then crush this herb into Lysander's eye,
Whose liquor hath this virtuous property
To take from thence all error with his might
And make his eyeballs roll with wonted sight.
370 When they next wake, all this derision
Shall seem a dream and fruitless vision.
And back to Athens shall the lovers wend,
With league whose date till death shall never end.
Whiles I in this affair do thee employ,
375 I'll to my queen and beg her Indian boy.
And then I will her charmèd eye release
From monster's view, and all things shall be peace.

ROBIN

Believe me, King of Illusions, I made a mistake. Didn't you tell me that I'd be able to recognize the man by the Athenian clothes he was wearing? So far I've done exactly what I was supposed to do—I put the love potion on an Athenian's eyes. And so far I'm pleased with the way things have turned out, since I find all of this commotion very entertaining.

OBERON

As you can see, these lovers are looking for a place to fight. Hurry up, Robin, and make the night dark and cloudy. Cover the sky with a low-hanging fog, as dark as hell, and get these overeager rivals so completely lost in the woods that they can't run into each other. Imitate Lysander's voice and egg Demetrius on with insults. Then rant for a while in Demetrius's voice, and egg Lysander on. That way you'll get them away from each other until they're so exhausted that they'll sleep like the dead. (OBERON *gives a new flower to* ROBIN) When they're asleep, crush some of this flower's juice into Lysander's eyes. The flower's juice has the power to erase all the damage that's been done to his eyes, and to make him see normally, the way he used to. When they wake up, all this trouble and conflict will seem like a dream or a meaningless vision. Then the lovers will go back to Athens, united together until death. While you're busy with that, I'll go see Queen Titania and ask her once again for the Indian boy. And then I'll undo the spell that I cast over her, so she won't be in love with that monster anymore. Then everything will be peaceful again.

ACT THREE

ROBIN
My fairy lord, this must be done with haste.
For night's swift dragons cut the clouds full fast,
380   And yonder shines Aurora's harbinger,
At whose approach, ghosts, wandering here and there,
Troop home to churchyards. Damnèd spirits all,
That in crossways and floods have burial,
Already to their wormy beds are gone.
385   For fear lest day should look their shames upon,
They willfully themselves exile from light
And must for aye consort with black-browed night.

OBERON
But we are spirits of another sort.
I with the morning's love have oft made sport,
390   And like a forester the groves may tread
Even till the eastern gate, all fiery red,
Opening on Neptune with fair blessèd beams,
Turns into yellow gold his salt green streams.
But notwithstanding, haste. Make no delay.
395   We may effect this business yet ere day.

Exit OBERON

ROBIN
Up and down, up and down,
I will lead them up and down.
I am feared in field and town.
Goblin, lead them up and down.
400   Here comes one.

Enter LYSANDER

LYSANDER
Where art thou, proud Demetrius? Speak thou now.

ROBIN

We've got to act fast, my lord of the fairies. Night's fading quickly, and in the distance the morning star is shining, warning us that dawn is coming. At dawn, the ghosts that have been wandering around all night go home to the graveyards. The souls of people who weren't buried in holy ground, but instead lie rotting by the side of the road or at the bottom of a river, have already gone back to their wormy graves. They weren't buried in a real graveyard because they committed suicide, and they don't want their shame to be seen in daylight, so they avoid sunlight and stay forever in the darkness of night.

OBERON

But we're not like that. We're a different kind of spirit, and we don't have to run away from the sunlight. I like the morning. I often wander around in the woods like a forest ranger until the sun rises in the fiery red sky over the ocean, turning the salty green water to gold. But you should hurry anyway. Don't delay. We still have time to get all of this done before daybreak.

OBERON *exits.*

ROBIN

Up and down, up and down,
I will lead them up and down.
The people fear me in the country and the town.
Goblin, lead them up and down.
Here comes one of them now.

LYSANDER *enters.*

LYSANDER

Where are you, Demetrius, you arrogant bastard? Say something.

ROBIN
> (*as* DEMETRIUS)
> Here, villain. Drawn and ready. Where art thou?

LYSANDER
> I will be with thee straight.

ROBIN
> (*as* DEMETRIUS)   Follow me then
> To plainer ground.

>   *Exit* LYSANDER

Enter DEMETRIUS

DEMETRIUS
>   Lysander, speak again!
405 Thou runaway, thou coward, art thou fled?
> Speak! In some bush? Where dost thou hide thy head?

ROBIN
> (*as* LYSANDER) Thou coward, art thou bragging to the stars,
> Telling the bushes that thou look'st for wars,
> And wilt not come? Come, recreant. Come, thou child!
410 I'll whip thee with a rod. He is defiled
> That draws a sword on thee.

DEMETRIUS
>   Yea, art thou there?

ROBIN
> (*as* LYSANDER)
> Follow my voice. We'll try no manhood here.

>   *Exeunt*

Enter LYSANDER

LYSANDER
> He goes before me and still dares me on.
> When I come where he calls, then he is gone.
415 The villain is much lighter-heeled than I.
> I followed fast, but faster he did fly,

ROBIN

(in DEMETRIUS's voice) I'm over here, you villain, with my sword out and ready to fight. Where are you?

LYSANDER

I'm coming.

ROBIN

(in DEMETRIUS's voice) Let's go to a flatter area where we can fight more easily.

LYSANDER *exits.*

DEMETRIUS *enters.*

DEMETRIUS

Lysander, say something! You coward, did you run away from me? Say something! Are you behind some bush? Where are you hiding?

ROBIN

(in LYSANDER's voice) You coward, are you bragging to the stars and telling the bushes that you want a fight, but then you won't come and fight me? Come here, you coward! Come here, you child! I'll beat you with a stick. It would be shameful to fight you with a sword, the way I would fight with a real man.

DEMETRIUS

Are you there?

ROBIN

(in LYSANDER's voice) Follow my voice. This isn't a good place to fight.

They exit.

LYSANDER *enters.*

LYSANDER

He's walking ahead of me, and he keeps daring me to follow him. When I reach the place he's calling from, he disappears. This villain is much quicker than I am. I ran after him fast, but he ran away from me faster, so

That fallen am I in dark uneven way,
And here will rest me.
(lies down)

                               Come, thou gentle day!
For if but once thou show me thy grey light,
420   I'll find Demetrius and revenge this spite.
(sleeps)

Enter ROBIN *and* DEMETRIUS

ROBIN
(as LYSANDER *to* DEMETRIUS*)*
Ho, ho, ho! Coward, why comest thou not?

DEMETRIUS
Abide me, if thou darest! For well I wot
Thou runn'st before me, shifting every place,
And darest not stand nor look me in the face.
425   Where art thou now?

ROBIN
(as LYSANDER*)*   Come hither. I am here.

DEMETRIUS
Nay, then, thou mock'st me. Thou shalt buy this dear
If ever I thy face by daylight see.
Now go thy way. Faintness constraineth me
To measure out my length on this cold bed.
430   By day's approach look to be visited.
(lies down and sleeps)

Enter HELENA

HELENA
O weary night, O long and tedious night,
Abate thy hours. Shine comforts from the east,
That I may back to Athens by daylight
From these that my poor company detest.
435   And sleep, that sometimes shuts up sorrow's eye,
Steal me awhile from mine own company.
(lies down and sleeps)

that now here I am in some dark part of the forest where the ground is uneven. I'll rest here. *(he lies down)* I hope the pleasant daytime comes soon! As soon as the gray light of early morning appears, I'll find Demetrius and get my revenge for this insult.

LYSANDER *lies down and falls asleep.* ROBIN *and* DEMETRIUS *enter.*

ROBIN

(in LYSANDER's *voice)* Ha, ha, ha! Hey, You coward, why aren't you coming?

DEMETRIUS

Wait for me, if you're not too scared! I know that's why you're running away from me, constantly changing places—you're afraid to stand still and wait for me. You're scared to look me in the eye. Where are you now?

ROBIN

(in LYSANDER's *voice)* Come here. I'm over here.

DEMETRIUS

No, you're just taunting me. You'll pay for this if I ever see you face-to-face in the daylight. Go wherever you want. I'm exhausted; I need to lie down and sleep on this cold ground. But watch out. I'll find you at dawn. *(*DEMETRIUS *lies down and sleeps)*

HELENA *enters.*

HELENA

Oh, what a long, tedious, exhausting night! I wish it would end. I wish the comforting light of day would shine so I can go back to Athens and get away from these people who hate me so much. I hope I'll be able to sleep and escape my troubles for a while. People can sometimes forget their difficulties when they're asleep. *(*HELENA *lies down and sleeps)*

ROBIN

Yet but three? Come one more.
Two of both kinds make up four.
Here she comes, cursed and sad.
440 Cupid is a knavish lad
Thus to make poor females mad.

Enter HERMIA

HERMIA

Never so weary, never so in woe,
Bedabbled with the dew and torn with briers,
I can no further crawl, no further go.
445 My legs can keep no pace with my desires.
Here will I rest me till the break of day.
Heavens shield Lysander if they mean a fray!
(lies down and sleeps)

ROBIN

On the ground
Sleep sound.
450 I'll apply
To your eye.
Gentle lover, remedy.
(squeezes flower juice into LYSANDER*'s eyes)*
When thou wakest,
Thou takest
455 True delight
In the sight
Of thy former lady's eye.
And the country proverb known—
That every man should take his own—
460 In your waking shall be shown.
Jack shall have Jill.
Nought shall go ill.
The man shall have his mare again, and all shall be well.

Exit ROBIN

ROBIN

Only three so far? We're still waiting for one more. Two of both kinds makes four. Ah, here she comes, angry and sad. Cupid is a bad boy for making poor women go crazy like this.

HERMIA *enters.*

HERMIA

I've never been more exhausted or upset. I'm all wet from the dew and scratched up by thorns, and I can't crawl any farther. I just can't go on. My legs can't hold themselves up. I'll sleep here until morning. If they do fight, I hope Lysander is safe! *(HERMIA lies down and sleeps)*

ROBIN

Sleep well there on the ground. I'll cure you, gentle lover, by putting this medicine on your eyes. *(ROBIN puts the nectar of the flower on LYSANDER's eyelids)* When you wake you will be truly delighted to see the woman you once loved. And when you wake up, you'll be a walking illustration of the well-known country proverb. "Jack will have Jill and everything will be all right."

ROBIN *exits.*

ACT FOUR

Scene 1

LYSANDER, DEMETRIUS, HELENA, *and* HERMIA *sleep. Enter* TITANIA, *Queen of the Fairies; and* BOTTOM, *with the ass's head; and fairies* PEASEBLOSSOM, COBWEB, MOTH, MUSTARDSEED; OBERON *the king behind them, unseen*

TITANIA
(to BOTTOM*)* Come, sit thee down upon this flowery bed
While I thy amiable cheeks do coy,
And stick musk roses in thy sleek, smooth head,
And kiss thy fair large ears, my gentle joy.

BOTTOM
5 Where's Peaseblossom?

PEASEBLOSSOM
Ready.

BOTTOM
Scratch my head, Peaseblossom. Where's Monsieur
Cobweb?

COBWEB
Ready.

BOTTOM
10 Monsieur Cobweb, good monsieur, get you your weapons
in your hand and kill me a red-hipped humble-bee on the
top of a thistle. And, good monsieur, bring me the honey
bag. Do not fret yourself too much in the action, monsieur.
And good monsieur, have a care the honey bag break not. I
15 would be loath to have you overflown with a honey bag,
signor.

Exit COBWEB

Where's Monsieur Mustardseed?

MUSTARDSEED
Ready.

ACT FOUR

Scene 1

DEMETRIUS, HELENA, HERMIA, and LYSANDER are still sleeping on the stage. TITANIA enters with BOTTOM, who still has a donkey's head, and the fairies PEASEBLOS-SOM, COBWEB, MOTH, and MUSTARDSEED. OBERON enters behind them, unseen by those onstage.

TITANIA

(to BOTTOM) Come over here and sit down on this flowery bed while I caress those lovable cheeks. I'll put roses on your silky, smooth head and kiss your big, beautiful ears, my gentle darling.

BOTTOM

Where's Peaseblossom?

PEASEBLOSSOM

Here.

BOTTOM

Scratch my head, Peaseblossom. Where's Monsieur Cobweb?

COBWEB

Here.

BOTTOM

Monsieur Cobweb, sir, get out your weapons and kill me a striped bumblebee on a thistle, and bring me its honey. Don't tire yourself out, monsieur. Oh, and monsieur, be careful not to break the honey-sac. I'd hate to see you drowned in honey, sir.

COBWEB exits.

Where's Monsieur Mustardseed?

MUSTARDSEED

Here.

BOTTOM
Give me your neaf, Monsieur Mustardseed. Pray you,
20   leave your courtesy, good monsieur.

MUSTARDSEED
What's your will?

BOTTOM
Nothing, good monsieur, but to help Cavalery Cobweb to
scratch. I must to the barber's, monsieur, for methinks I am
marvelous hairy about the face. And I am such a tender ass,
25   if my hair do but tickle me, I must scratch.

TITANIA
What, wilt thou hear some music, my sweet love?

BOTTOM
I have a reasonable good ear in music. Let's have the tongs
and the bones.

TITANIA
Or say, sweet love, what thou desirest to eat.

BOTTOM
30   Truly, a peck of provender. I could munch your good dry
oats. Methinks I have a great desire to a bottle of hay. Good
hay, sweet hay, hath no fellow.

TITANIA
I have a venturous fairy that shall seek
The squirrel's hoard and fetch thee new nuts.

BOTTOM
35   I had rather have a handful or two of dried peas. But, I pray
you, let none of your people stir me. I have an exposition of
sleep come upon me.

TITANIA
Sleep thou, and I will wind thee in my arms.
Fairies, be gone, and be all ways away.

Exeunt **FAIRIES**

BOTTOM

Give me your first, Mr. Mustardseed. Please, stop bowing, good sir.

MUSTARDSEED

What would you like me to do?

BOTTOM

Nothing, good sir, except to help Sir Cobweb scratch my head. I should go to the barber's, monsieur, because I think I'm getting really hairy around the face. And I'm such a sensitive ass that if my hair even tickles me a little, I need to scratch.

TITANIA

Would you like to hear some music, my sweet love?

BOTTOM

I have a pretty good ear for music. Let's hear someone play the triangle and the sticks.

TITANIA

Or tell me, my sweet love, what you'd like to eat.

BOTTOM

Actually, I'd like a few pounds of grass. I'd like to munch on some good dry oats. Or maybe I've got a hankering for a bundle of hay. There's nothing like good hay, really sweet hay.

TITANIA

I have an adventurous fairy who'll go seek out the squirrel's secret stash and get you some fresh nuts.

BOTTOM

I'd rather have a handful or two of dried peas. But please don't let any of your people wake me up. I really want to sleep now.

TITANIA

Go to sleep, and I will wrap my arms around you. Fairies, go away. Run off in all directions.

The FAIRIES *exit.*

40   So doth the woodbine the sweet honeysuckle
      Gently entwist. The female ivy so
      Enrings the barky fingers of the elm.
      Oh, how I love thee! How I dote on thee!

      TITANIA *and* BOTTOM *sleep*
      Enter ROBIN

OBERON
      Welcome, good Robin. Seest thou this sweet sight?
45   Her dotage now I do begin to pity.
      For, meeting her of late behind the wood,
      Seeking sweet favors from this hateful fool,
      I did upbraid her and fall out with her.
      For she his hairy temples then had rounded
50   With a coronet of fresh and fragrant flowers,
      And that same dew, which sometime on the buds
      Was wont to swell like round and orient pearls,
      Stood now within the pretty flowerets' eyes
      Like tears that did their own disgrace bewail.
55   When I had at my pleasure taunted her
      And she in mild terms begged my patience,
      I then did ask of her her changeling child,
      Which straight she gave me and her fairy sent
      To bear him to my bower in Fairyland.
60   And now I have the boy, I will undo
      This hateful imperfection of her eyes.
      And, gentle Puck, take this transformèd scalp
      From off the head of this Athenian swain,
      That, he awaking when the other do,
65   May all to Athens back again repair
      And think no more of this night's accidents
      But as the fierce vexation of a dream.
      But first I will release the fairy queen.
      (*squeezing flower juice into* TITANIA*'s eyes*)

I'm putting my arms around you just like the woodbine tendril gently twists itself around the sweet honeysuckle, and like the female ivy curls itself around the branches of the elm tree. Oh, how I love you! I'm so crazy about you!

BOTTOM *and* TITANIA *sleep.* ROBIN *enters.*

OBERON

Welcome, good Robin. Do you see this sweet sight? Now I'm starting to pity Titania for being so infatuated. I ran into her recently at the edge of the forest, looking for sweet presents for this hateful idiot, and I scolded her and argued with her. She had put a wreath of fresh, fragrant flowers around his hairy forehead, and the drops of dew that lay in the center of the flowers made the flowers look like they were crying with shame to be decorating the head of that ugly jackass. When I had taunted her as much as I wanted to, and she begged me very nicely to leave her alone, I asked her for the stolen Indian child. She said yes right away, and sent a fairy to bring him to my home in Fairyland. And now that I have the boy, I'll undo the spell that makes her vision so disgustingly wrong. And, gentle Puck, take this transformed ass's head off of the head of that Athenian man, so that when he wakes up at the same time as the rest of them do, they can all go back to Athens. They'll only remember the events of tonight as a very unpleasant dream. But first I'll release the fairy queen from the spell.
(OBERON *squeezes the juice from the second flower into* TITANIA*'s eyes*)

Be as thou wast wont to be.
70   See as thou wast wont to see.
Dian's bud o'er Cupid's flower
Hath such force and blessèd power.
Now, my Titania, wake you, my sweet queen.

TITANIA
(waking) My Oberon, what visions have I seen!
75   Methought I was enamored of an ass.

OBERON
There lies your love.

TITANIA
                              How came these things to pass?
Oh, how mine eyes do loathe his visage now!

OBERON
Silence awhile.—Robin, take off this head.—
Titania, music call, and strike more dead
80   Than common sleep of all these five the sense.

TITANIA
Music, ho! Music such as charmeth sleep!

Music

ROBIN
(taking the ass's head off BOTTOM*)*
Now when thou wakest, with thine own fool's eyes peep.

OBERON
Sound, music!—Come, my queen, take hands with me,
And rock the ground whereon these sleepers be.
(dances with TITANIA*)*
85   Now thou and I are new in amity,
And will tomorrow midnight solemnly
Dance in Duke Theseus' house triumphantly,
And bless it to all fair prosperity.
There shall the pairs of faithful lovers be
90   Wedded, with Theseus, all in jollity.

Be like you used to be, and see like you used to see.
This bud belongs to Diana, the goddess of virginity,
and it has the power to undo the effects of Cupid's
flower. Now, Titania, wake up, my sweet queen.

TITANIA

(waking up) Oberon, I've had such a strange dream! I
dreamed I was in love with an ass.

OBERON

There's your boyfriend, sleeping right over there.

TITANIA

How did this happen? Oh, I hate looking at his face
now!

OBERON

Be quiet for a while.—Robin, take off his donkey
head.—Titania, get the fairies to play some music,
and make these five people sleep more soundly than
humans have ever slept before.

TITANIA

Music! Play the kind of music that puts people to
sleep.

The music plays.

ROBIN

(removing the ass's head from BOTTOM*)* When you wake
up, see things with your own foolish eyes again.

OBERON

Play the music.—Take my hands, my queen, and
we'll lull these people to sleep with our soft dancing.
(he dances with TITANIA*)* Now that you and I are
friends again, we can dance for Duke Theseus tomorrow at midnight, and bless his marriage and his marriage bed. These other lovers will get married
alongside him, and they'll all be in high spirits.

ROBIN
> Fairy King, attend, and mark.
> I do hear the morning lark.

OBERON
> Then, my queen, in silence sad,
> Trip we after the night's shade.
95 > We the globe can compass soon
> Swifter than the wandering moon.

TITANIA
> Come, my lord, and in our flight
> Tell me how it came this night
> That I sleeping here was found
100 > With these mortals on the ground.

>> *Exeunt* OBERON, TITANIA, *and* ROBIN
> *Wind horn within*
> *Enter* THESEUS *and all his train,* EGEUS, *and* HIPPOLYTA

THESEUS
> Go, one of you, find out the forester.
> For now our observation is performed.
> And since we have the vaward of the day,
> My love shall hear the music of my hounds.
105 > Uncouple in the western valley. Let them go.
> Dispatch, I say, and find the forester.

>> *Exit one of the train*

> We will, fair queen, up to the mountain's top,
> And mark the musical confusion
> Of hounds and echo in conjunction.

HIPPOLYTA
110 > I was with Hercules and Cadmus once,
> When in a wood of Crete they bayed the bear
> With hounds of Sparta. Never did I hear
> Such gallant chiding. For, besides the groves,

ROBIN

Listen, Fairy King. I can hear the lark singing. Morning's here.

OBERON

In that case, my queen, let's travel silently and solemnly across the globe to where it's still night, circling the earth faster than the moon does.

TITANIA

While we're walking, you can tell me how I ended up sleeping on the ground with these humans last night.

OBERON, TITANIA, *and* ROBIN *exit.*

A hunting horn blows. THESEUS *enters with his servants,* EGEUS *and* HIPPOLYTA.

THESEUS

One of you go find the forest ranger. Since we're done with the May Day rites and it's still so early in the morning, my love will have a chance to hear the beautiful music of my hunting dogs barking as they chase their prey. Unleash the dogs in the western valley. Let them go. Now go find the forest ranger.

A servant exits.

My beautiful queen, we'll go up the mountain and listen to the hounds as their barking echoes in the cliffs and sounds like music.

HIPPOLYTA

I was with the heroes Hercules and Cadmus once, when their Spartan hunting dogs cornered a bear. I'd never heard such impressive barking before. The forests, the skies, the mountains, everything around us

The skies, the fountains, every region near
115 Seemed all one mutual cry. I never heard
So musical a discord, such sweet thunder.

THESEUS
My hounds are bred out of the Spartan kind,
So flewed, so sanded, and their heads are hung
With ears that sweep away the morning dew,
120 Crook-kneed, and dew-lapped like Thessalian bulls,
Slow in pursuit, but matched in mouth like bells,
Each under each. A cry more tunable
Was never hollaed to, nor cheered with horn,
In Crete, in Sparta, nor in Thessaly.
125 Judge when you hear.
(sees the four sleeping lovers)
               But, soft! What nymphs are these?

EGEUS
My lord, this is my daughter here asleep.
And this, Lysander. This Demetrius is.
This Helena, old Nedar's Helena.
I wonder of their being here together.

THESEUS
130 No doubt they rose up early to observe
The rite of May, and hearing our intent
Came here in grace our solemnity.
But speak, Egeus. Is not this the day
That Hermia should give answer of her choice?

EGEUS
135 It is, my lord.

THESEUS
Go, bid the huntsmen wake them with their horns.

                      Exit one of the train

Wind horns and shout within
LYSANDER, **DEMETRIUS**, **HELENA**, *and* **HERMIA** *wake and
start up*

seemed to echo the barks of the hounds. I'd never heard such raucous music, such pleasant thunder.

THESEUS

My dogs are bred from Spartan hounds. They have the same folds of flesh around their mouths, the same sandy-colored fur, and hanging ears that brush the morning dew off the grass. They have crooked knees and folds of skin under their necks, just like the Spartan hounds. They're not very fast in the chase, but their barking sounds like bells ringing. Each bark is perfectly in tune with the others, like notes on a scale. No one, anywhere, has ever gone hunting with a more musical pack of dogs. Judge for yourself when you hear them. *(he sees the four lovers sleeping)* But wait a minute! Who are these women?

EGEUS

My lord, that's my daughter asleep on the ground over there, and this is Lysander here, and this is Demetrius, and this is Helena, old Nedar's daughter. I don't understand why they're all here together.

THESEUS

They probably woke up early to celebrate May Day and came here for my celebration when they heard I'd be here. But tell me, Egeus. Isn't today the day when Hermia has to tell us her decision about whether she'll marry Demetrius?

EGEUS

It is, my lord.

THESEUS

Go tell the hunters to blow their horns and wake them up.

A servant exits.

Someone shouts offstage. Horns are blown. LYSANDER, DEMETRIUS, HELENA, *and* HERMIA, *wake up.*

ACT FOUR

Good morrow, friends. Saint Valentine is past.
Begin these woodbirds but to couple now?

LYSANDER, DEMETRIUS, HELENA, *and* HERMIA *kneel*

LYSANDER
Pardon, my lord.
THESEUS
                I pray you all, stand up.

LYSANDER, DEMETRIUS, HELENA, *and* HERMIA *stand*

(to LYSANDER *and* DEMETRIUS*)*
140   I know you two are rival enemies.
How comes this gentle concord in the world,
That hatred is so far from jealousy
To sleep by hate and fear no enmity?

LYSANDER
My lord, I shall reply amazèdly,
145   Half sleep, half waking. But as yet, I swear,
I cannot truly say how I came here.
But as I think—for truly would I speak,
And now do I bethink me, so it is—
I came with Hermia hither. Our intent
150   Was to be gone from Athens, where we might,
Without the peril of the Athenian law—

EGEUS
(to THESEUS*)* Enough, enough, my lord. You have enough!
I beg the law, the law, upon his head.—
They would have stol'n away, they would, Demetrius,
155   Thereby to have defeated you and me,
You of your wife and me of my consent,
Of my consent that she should be your wife.

DEMETRIUS
(to THESEUS*)* My lord, fair Helen told me of their stealth,
Of this their purpose hither to this wood.

Good morning, my friends. Valentine's Day is over. Are you lovebirds only starting to pair up now?

LYSANDER, DEMETRIUS, HELENA, *and* HERMIA *all kneel.*

LYSANDER

Forgive us, my lord.

THESEUS

Please, all of you, stand up.

LYSANDER, DEMETRIUS, HELENA, *and* HERMIA *get up.*

(to LYSANDER *and* DEMETRIUS*)* I know you two are enemies. Has the world really become so gentle and peaceful that people who hate each other have started to trust each other and sleep beside each other without being afraid?

LYSANDER

My lord, what I say may be a little confused, since I'm half asleep and half awake. I swear, at the moment I really couldn't tell you how I ended up here. But I think—I want to tell you the truth, and now that I think about it, I think this is true—I came here with Hermia. We were planning to leave Athens to escape the Athenian law and—

EGEUS

(to THESEUS*)* Enough, enough, my lord. You've heard enough evidence! I insist that the law punish him— They were going to run away, Demetrius, they were running away to defeat us, robbing you of your wife and me of my fatherly right to decide who my son-in-law will be.

DEMETRIUS

(to THESEUS*)* My lord, the beautiful Helena told me about their secret plan to escape into this forest. I was

160   And I in fury hither followed them,
       Fair Helena in fancy following me.
       But, my good lord, I wot not by what power—
       But by some power it is—my love to Hermia,
       Melted as the snow, seems to me now
165   As the remembrance of an idle gaud
       Which in my childhood I did dote upon.
       And all the faith, the virtue of my heart,
       The object and the pleasure of mine eye,
       Is only Helena. To her, my lord,
170   Was I betrothed ere I saw Hermia.
       But like in sickness did I loathe this food.
       But as in health, come to my natural taste,
       Now I do wish it, love it, long for it,
       And will for evermore be true to it.

THESEUS
175   Fair lovers, you are fortunately met.
       Of this discourse we more will hear anon.—
       Egeus, I will overbear your will.
       For in the temple by and by with us
       These couples shall eternally be knit.—
180   And, for the morning now is something worn,
       Our purposed hunting shall be set aside.
       Away with us to Athens. Three and three,
       We'll hold a feast in great solemnity.
       Come, Hippolyta.

                    Exeunt THESEUS, HIPPOLYTA, EGEUS, *and train*

DEMETRIUS
185   These things seem small and undistinguishable,
       Like far-off mountains turnèd into clouds.

HERMIA
       Methinks I see these things with parted eye,
       When everything seems double.

furious and followed them here, and the lovely Helena was so in love with me that she followed me. I'm not sure how it happened—but somehow, something made my love for Hermia melt away like snow. My past love for Hermia now seems like a memory of some cheap toy I used to love as a child. Now the only person I love, and believe in, and want to look at, is Helena. I was engaged to her before I ever met Hermia. Then I hated her for a time, as a sick person hates the food he usually loves. But now I have my natural taste back, like a sick person when he recovers. Now I want Helena, I love her, I long for her, and I will always be true to her.

THESEUS

You pretty lovers are lucky you met me here. We'll talk more about this later.—Egeus, I'm overriding your wishes. These couples will be married along with me and Hippolyta in the temple later today.—And now, since the morning is almost over, we'll give up on the idea of hunting. Come with us to Athens. We three couples will celebrate with a sumptuous feast. Come, Hippolyta.

THESEUS, HIPPOLYTA, and EGEUS exit with their followers.

DEMETRIUS

What exactly just happened? The events of last night seem small and hard to see clearly, like far-off mountains that look like clouds in the distance.

HERMIA

Yes, it's like my eyes are out of focus, and I'm seeing everything double.

HELENA
                                    So methinks.
          And I have found Demetrius like a jewel,
190   Mine own, and not mine own.

DEMETRIUS
                                    Are you sure
          That we are awake? It seems to me
          That yet we sleep, we dream. Do not you think
          The duke was here, and bid us follow him?

HERMIA
          Yea, and my father.

HELENA
                    And Hippolyta.

LYSANDER
195   And he did bid us follow to the temple.

DEMETRIUS
          Why then, we are awake. Let's follow him
          And by the way let us recount our dreams.

          Exeunt LYSANDER, DEMETRIUS, HELENA, *and* HERMIA

BOTTOM
          (waking) When my cue comes, call me, and I will answer.
          My next is "Most fair Pyramus." Heigh-ho! Peter Quince?
200.   Flute the bellows-mender? Snout the tinker? Starveling?
          God's my life, stol'n hence, and left me asleep? I have had
          a most rare vision. I have had a dream—past the wit of man
          to say what dream it was. Man is but an ass if he go about
          to expound this dream. Methought I was—there is no man
205.   can tell what. Methought I was, and methought I had—but
          man is but a patched fool if he will offer to say what
          methought I had. The eye of man hath not heard, the ear of
          man hath not seen, man's hand is not able to taste, his
          tongue to conceive, nor his heart to report what my dream
210   was. I will get Peter Quince to write a ballad of this dream.

HELENA

Me too. I won Demetrius so easily, as if he were a precious diamond I just found lying around. It's mine because I found it, but I feel like someone else could easily come and claim it was hers.

DEMETRIUS

Are you sure we're awake? It seems to me like we're still sleeping, still dreaming. Do you remember seeing the duke here? Did he tell us to follow him?

HERMIA

Yes, he did. And my father was here too.

HELENA

And Hippolyta.

LYSANDER

And he told us to follow him to the temple.

DEMETRIUS

Well, then, we're awake. Let's follow him. We can tell one another our dreams along the way.

LYSANDER, DEMETRIUS, HELENA, *and* HERMIA *exit.*

BOTTOM

(waking up) Tell me when my cue comes, and I'll say my line. My next cue is "Most handsome Pyramus." Hey! Peter Quince? Flute the bellows-repairman? Snout the handyman? Starveling? My God, they've all run away and left me sleeping here? What a weird dream I had.—You can't even describe such a weird dream. You'd be an ass if you even tried to explain it. I thought I was—no, nobody can even describe what I was. I thought I was, I thought I had—but a person would be an idiot to try to say what I thought I had. No eye has ever heard, no ear has ever seen, no hand has tasted, or tongue felt, or heart described what my dream was like. I'll get Peter Quince to write this

ACT FOUR

It shall be called "Bottom's Dream" because it hath no
bottom. And I will sing it in the latter end of a play before
the duke. Peradventure, to make it the more gracious, I
shall sing it at her death.

Exit

dream down as a ballad. I'll call it "Bottom's Dream" because it's so deep that it has no bottom. And I'll sing it for the duke in the intermission of a play. Or maybe, to make it even more lovely, I'll sing it when the heroine dies.

BOTTOM *exits.*

ACT FOUR, Scene 2

Enter QUINCE, FLUTE, SNOUT, *and* STARVELING

QUINCE
Have you sent to Bottom's house? Is he come home yet?

STARVELING
He cannot be heard of. Out of doubt he is transported.

FLUTE
If he come not, then the play is marred. It goes not forward.
Doth it?

QUINCE
5   It is not possible. You have not a man in all Athens able to
discharge Pyramus but he.

FLUTE
No, he hath simply the best wit of any handicraft man in
Athens.

QUINCE
Yea, and the best person too. And he is a very paramour for
10   a sweet voice.

FLUTE
You must say "paragon." A "paramour" is, God bless us, a
thing of naught.

Enter SNUG

SNUG
Masters, the duke is coming from the temple, and there is
two or three lords and ladies more married. If our sport had
15   gone forward, we had all been made men.

FLUTE
O sweet bully Bottom! Thus hath he lost sixpence a day
during his life. He could not have 'scaped sixpence a day.
An the duke had not given him sixpence a day for playing

ACT FOUR, Scene 2

QUINCE, FLUTE, SNOUT, *and* STARVELING *enter.*

QUINCE

Have you sent anyone to Bottom's house? Has he come home yet?

STARVELING

No one's heard from him. I'm sure he's been kidnapped.

FLUTE

If he doesn't show up, the play is ruined. It won't go on. Will it?

QUINCE

No, it would be impossible. He's the only person in Athens who can play Pyramus.

FLUTE

Definitely. He's quite simply the smartest workingman in Athens.

QUINCE

Yes, and the best looking too. And his voice is the paramour of sweetness.

FLUTE

You mean "paragon." A "paramour" is something bad.

paramour = lover

SNUG *enters.*

SNUG

The duke's leaving the temple. Two or three more lords and ladies have been married too. If we'd been able to put on our play, we would have had it made.

FLUTE

Oh that great, funny guy, Bottom! He would have gotten a pension of six pence a day for his whole life. Six pence a day would've been forced on him. I'll be damned if the duke wouldn't have given him six pence

20 Pyramus, I'll be hanged. He would have deserved it.
Sixpence a day in Pyramus, or nothing.

Enter BOTTOM

BOTTOM
Where are these lads? Where are these hearts?

QUINCE
Bottom! O most courageous day! O most happy hour!

BOTTOM
Masters, I am to discourse wonders—but ask me not what,
for if I tell you I am no true Athenian. I will tell you
25 everything, right as it fell out.

QUINCE
Let us hear, sweet Bottom.

BOTTOM
Not a word of me. All that I will tell you is that the duke
hath dined. Get your apparel together, good strings to your
beards, new ribbons to your pumps. Meet presently at the
30 palace. Every man look o'er his part. For the short and the
long is, our play is preferred. In any case, let Thisbe have
clean linen. And let not him that plays the lion pair his nails,
for they shall hang out for the lion's claws. And most dear
actors, eat no onions nor garlic, for we are to utter sweet
35 breath. And I do not doubt but to hear them say, "It is a
sweet comedy." No more words. Away, go away!

Exeunt

a day for playing Pyramus. And he would have deserved it too. Pyramus is worth six pence a day, or it's worth nothing!

A pension of six pence a day would be a lot of money for a working class man.

BOTTOM *enters.*

BOTTOM

Where are my guys? Where are my good fellows?

QUINCE

Bottom! Oh, how wonderful to see you! Oh, what a relief!

BOTTOM

My friends, I've got some amazing things to tell you—but don't ask me to tell you what. I swear by my Athenian citizenship that I won't tell you anything. I'll tell you everything exactly as it happened.

QUINCE

Tell us, Bottom.

BOTTOM

No, you won't get a word out of me. All I'll tell you is that the duke has had dinner already. Now it's time to get your costumes together. Find some good strings for tying on your false beards, and grab new ribbons to decorate your shoes. Meet me at the palace as soon as possible. Look over your lines again. Our play's going to be performed for the duke! So make sure Thisbe's wearing clean underwear, and make sure whoever's playing the lion doesn't cut his nails, because he needs them long to look like lion's claws. And no one eat any onions or garlic. If we have sweet-smelling breath, I'm sure they'll say "it's a sweet play." Now no more talking. Get busy, go!

They all exit.

ACT FOUR

ACT FIVE

Scene 1

Enter THESEUS, HIPPOLYTA, *and* PHILOSTRATE, *with other attendant lords*

HIPPOLYTA
'Tis strange, my Theseus, that these lovers speak of.

THESEUS
More strange than true. I never may believe
These antique fables nor these fairy toys.
Lovers and madmen have such seething brains,
5   Such shaping fantasies, that apprehend
More than cool reason ever comprehends.
The lunatic, the lover, and the poet
Are of imagination all compact.
One sees more devils than vast hell can hold—
10   That is the madman. The lover, all as frantic,
Sees Helen's beauty in a brow of Egypt.
The poet's eye, in fine frenzy rolling,
Doth glance from heaven to Earth, from Earth to heaven.
And as imagination bodies forth
15   The forms of things unknown, the poet's pen
Turns them to shapes and gives to airy nothing
A local habitation and a name.
Such tricks hath strong imagination,
That if it would but apprehend some joy,
20   It comprehends some bringer of that joy.
Or in the night, imagining some fear,
How easy is a bush supposed a bear!

HIPPOLYTA
But all the story of the night told over,
And all their minds transfigured so together,
25   More witnesseth than fancy's images
And grows to something of great constancy,
But, howsoever, strange and admirable.

ACT FIVE

Scene 1

THESEUS, HIPPOLYTA, *and* PHILOSTRATE *enter, with a number of lords and servants.*

HIPPOLYTA

These lovers are saying some strange things, Theseus.

THESEUS

Yes, strange—and totally made up too. I'll never believe any of these old legends or fairy tales. Lovers and madmen hallucinate about things that sane people just can't understand. Lunatics, lovers, and poets all are ruled by their overactive imaginations. some people think they see devils and monsters everywhere—and they're lunatics. Lovers are just as crazy, and think a dark-skinned gypsy is the most gorgeous woman in the world. Poets are always looking around like they're having a fit, confusing the mundane with the otherworldly, and describing things in their writing that simply don't exist. All these people have such strong imaginations that, when they feel happy, they assume a god or some other supernatural being is bringing that happiness to them. Or if they're afraid of something at night, they look at the shrubbery and imagine it's a wild bear!

HIPPOLYTA

But the story that these lovers are telling, and the fact that they all saw and heard exactly the same things, make me think there's more going on here than imaginary fantasies. Their story is bizarre and astounding, but it's solid and consistent.

Enter lovers: LYSANDER, DEMETRIUS, HELENA, *and* HERMIA

THESEUS
 Here come the lovers, full of joy and mirth.—
 Joy, gentle friends! Joy and fresh days of love
30 Accompany your hearts!

LYSANDER
        More than to us
 Wait in your royal walks, your board, your bed!

THESEUS
 Come now, what masques, what dances shall we have
 To wear away this long age of three hours
 Between our after-supper and bedtime?
35 Where is our usual manager of mirth?
 What revels are in hand? Is there no play,
 To ease the anguish of a torturing hour?
 Call Philostrate.

PHILOSTRATE
      Here, mighty Theseus.

THESEUS
 Say, what abridgement have you for this evening?
40 What masque, what music? How shall we beguile
 The lazy time if not with some delight?

PHILOSTRATE
 (giving THESEUS *a document)*
 There is a brief, how many sports are ripe.
 Make choice of which your highness will see first.

THESEUS
 (reads)
    "The battle with the Centaurs, to be sung
45   By an Athenian eunuch to the harp."
 We'll none of that. That have I told my love,
 In glory of my kinsman Hercules.
    "The riot of the tipsy Bacchanals,
    Tearing the Thracian singer in their rage."
50 That is an old device, and it was played
 When I from Thebes came last a conqueror.

The lovers—LYSANDER, DEMETRIUS, HELENA, *and* HERMIA—*enter.*

THESEUS

Here come the lovers, laughing happily.—I wish you joy, my friends! I hope the days ahead are full of joy for you.

LYSANDER

We wish you even more joy, and hope joy comes to you in your royal walks, at your table, and in your royal bed!

THESEUS

Now, what kind of entertainment do we have to fill up the long three hours between dinner and bedtime? Where is our entertainment director? What performances have been prepared? Aren't there any plays for us to enjoy while we wait in torture for bedtime to come? Let me see Philostrate.

PHILOSTRATE

Here I am, Theseus.

THESEUS

Tell us what entertainment you've prepared for the evening. Which plays, what music? How will we pass the time without some entertainment?

PHILOSTRATE

(giving THESEUS *a piece of paper)* Here's a list of all of the acts that have been prepared. Choose which one you want to see first.

THESEUS

(reading) "The battle between Hercules and the Centaurs, to be sung by an Athenian eunuch, accompanied by a harp." No, we won't see that. I've already told that story to Hippolyta, while praising my cousin Hercules. What else? "The riot of the drunk Bacchanals who rip the singer Orpheus to shreds." That's an old show, and I saw it the last time I came back from

ACT FIVE

        "The thrice three Muses mourning for the death
        Of learning, late deceased in beggary."
That is some satire, keen and critical,
55   Not sorting with a nuptial ceremony.
        "A tedious brief scene of young Pyramus
        And his love Thisbe. Very tragical mirth."
"Merry" and "tragical"? "Tedious" and "brief"?
That is hot ice and wondrous strange snow.
60   How shall we find the concord of this discord?

PHILOSTRATE
A play there is, my lord, some ten words long,
Which is as brief as I have known a play.
But by ten words, my lord, it is too long,
Which makes it tedious. For in all the play
65   There is not one word apt, one player fitted.
And tragical, my noble lord, it is.
For Pyramus therein doth kill himself.
Which, when I saw rehearsed, I must confess,
Made mine eyes water—but more merry tears
70   The passion of loud laughter never shed.

THESEUS
What are they that do play it?

PHILOSTRATE
Hard-handed men that work in Athens here,
Which never labored in their minds till now,
And now have toiled their unbreathed memories
75   With this same play against your nuptial.

THESEUS
And we will hear it.

PHILOSTRATE
        No, my noble lord.
It is not for you. I have heard it over,
And it is nothing, nothing in the world—
Unless you can find sport in their intents,
80   Extremely stretched and conned with cru 'l pain
To do you service.

conquering Thebes. "The nine Muses mourning the death of learning and scholarship." That's some sharp, critical satire, and it's not appropriate for a wedding. "A tedious short drama about young Pyramus and his love Thisbe, a very sad and tragic comedy." A sad comedy? Short but still tedious? That's like hot ice and strange snow. How can this drama be so many contradictory things?

PHILOSTRATE

It's a play about ten words long, which is the shortest play I've ever heard of. But in my opinion, it's about ten words too long. That's why it's tedious. In the entire play, not one word is well-written, and not one of the actors is right for his part. It's tragic because Pyramus kills himself. I have to admit that when I saw his suicide during rehearsal, I had tears in my eyes— but they were tears of laughter.

THESEUS

Who are the actors?

PHILOSTRATE

Rough workmen from Athens who never spent much time thinking. Now they've worn out their out-of-shape brains to put on this play for your wedding.

THESEUS

So let's see it.

PHILOSTRATE

No, my noble lord. This play isn't right for you. I've seen the whole thing, and it's completely worthless— unless you think their bad acting and their misremembered lines—which they memorized so painfully—are funny.

THESEUS
I will hear that play.
For never anything can be amiss
When simpleness and duty tender it.
Go, bring them in.—And take your places, ladies.

Exit PHILOSTRATE

HIPPOLYTA
85   I love not to see wretchedness o'er charged
And duty in his service perishing.

THESEUS
Why, gentle sweet, you shall see no such thing.

HIPPOLYTA
He says they can do nothing in this kind.

THESEUS
The kinder we, to give them thanks for nothing.
90   Our sport shall be to take what they mistake.
And what poor duty cannot do, noble respect
Takes it in might, not merit.
Where I have come, great clerks have purposèd
To greet me with premeditated welcomes,
95   Where I have seen them shiver and look pale,
Make periods in the midst of sentences,
Throttle their practiced accent in their fears,
And in conclusion dumbly have broke off,
Not paying me a welcome. Trust me, sweet,
100   Out of this silence yet I picked a welcome,
And in the modesty of fearful duty
I read as much as from the rattling tongue
Of saucy and audacious eloquence.
Love, therefore, and tongue-tied simplicity
105   In least speak most, to my capacity.

Enter PHILOSTRATE

THESEUS

> I'll watch this play. Nothing can really be bad when it's created by simple people who try hard. Come on, bring them in. And sit down, ladies.

PHILOSTRATE *exits.*

HIPPOLYTA

> I don't like seeing poor people overburdened or looking bad when they're trying to do something good.

THESEUS

> You won't see anything like that, sweetheart.

HIPPOLYTA

> He just said that they're no good at acting.

THESEUS

> Then we're even kinder people for thanking them for something that they're not good at. We'll entertain ourselves by accepting their mistakes. When poor dutiful people can't do certain things well, generous people can consider the effort they put into it rather than the effect that they produce. In my travels, great scholars have come up to me, meaning to greet me with well-rehearsed welcoming speeches, and I have seen them tremble and turn pale, and pause inappropriately in the middle of their sentences, and botch their well-rehearsed tones of voice because they're so nervous, and then break off abruptly at the end, without actually welcoming me. Trust me, my sweet, I figured out that they were trying to welcome me even though they were silent, and that message was as clear from someone who was modest and nervously dutiful as it is from someone who is loud and audacious and eloquent. Therefore, love and tongue-tied simplicity can say the most even when they're saying the least, in my opinion.

PHILOSTRATE
So please your grace, the Prologue is addressed.

THESEUS
Let him approach.

Enter QUINCE *as the* PROLOGUE

PROLOGUE
(delivered by QUINCE*)*
If we offend, it is with our good will.
That you should think we come not to offend,
110   But with good will. To show our simple skill,
That is the true beginning of our end.
Consider then we come but in despite.
We do not come as minding to contest you,
Our true intent is. All for your delight
115   We are not here. That you should here repent you,
The actors are at hand, and by their show
You shall know all that you are like to know.

THESEUS
This fellow doth not stand upon points.

LYSANDER
He hath rid his prologue like a rough colt. He knows not the
120   stop. A good moral, my lord: it is not enough to speak, but
to speak true.

HIPPOLYTA
Indeed he hath played on his prologue like a child on a
recorder—a sound, but not in government.

PHILOSTRATE

Your grace, the person who is going to deliver the prologue is ready.

THESEUS

Let him come forward.

The PROLOGUE *(*QUINCE*) enters.*

PROLOGUE

If Quince had read this speech with the proper punctuation, it would mean "If we happen to offend you, we hope you know that we didn't come here intending to offend you, but with the good intention of showing off our little bit of skill. That's all we want to do. Please keep in mind that we came here only to please you. Our true intention is to delight you. We didn't come here to make you sorry. The actors are ready . . ."

If we happen to offend you, it's because we want to. We don't want you to think we came here to offend you, except that we want to offend you with our good intentions. Our plan to show off our little bit of talent will wind up getting us executed. Please keep in mind we're only here out of spite. We don't come here with the intention of making you happy. We're absolutely not here to delight you. The actors are ready to come out and make you sorry. By watching their show, you'll find out everything you're likely to know.

THESEUS

This guy doesn't pay much attention to punctuation.

LYSANDER

He rode that prologue like a wild horse. He didn't know how to stop it. The moral of this story is that it's not enough to speak; you have to speak grammatically.

HIPPOLYTA

Yes, he performed his prologue like a child plays a recorder—he can make sounds, but they're out of control.

THESEUS

His speech was like a tangled chain. Nothing impaired, but
125   all disordered. Who is next?

Enter BOTTOM *as* PYRAMUS,
and FLUTE *as* THISBE,
and SNOUT *as* WALL,
and STARVELING *as* MOONSHINE,
and SNUG *as* LION

PROLOGUE

(delivered by QUINCE*)*

Gentles, perchance you wonder at this show.
But wonder on, till truth make all things plain.
This man is Pyramus, if you would know.
This beauteous lady Thisbe is certain.
130   This man, with lime and roughcast, doth present
Wall, that vile wall which did these lovers sunder.
And through Wall's chink, poor souls, they are content
To whisper. At the which let no man wonder.
This man, with lanthorn, dog, and bush of thorn,
135   Presenteth Moonshine. For, if you will know,
By moonshine did these lovers think no scorn
To meet at Ninus' tomb—there, there to woo.
This grisly beast, which "Lion" hight by name,
The trusty Thisbe, coming first by night,
140   Did scare away, or rather did affright.
And, as she fled, her mantle she did fall,
Which Lion vile with bloody mouth did stain.
Anon comes Pyramus, sweet youth and tall,
And finds his trusty Thisbe's mantle slain.
145   Whereat, with blade, with bloody blameful blade,
He bravely broached his boiling bloody breast.
And Thisbe, tarrying in mulberry shade,
His dagger drew, and died. For all the rest,
Let Lion, Moonshine, Wall, and lovers twain
150   At large discourse, while here they do remain.

THESEUS

His speech was like a tangled chain. It went on and on and was a total mess. Who's next?

BOTTOM enters as PYRAMUS, with FLUTE as THISBE, SNOUT as WALL, STARVELING as MOONSHINE, and SNUG as LION.

PROLOGUE

(delivered by QUINCE) Ladies and gentlemen, perhaps you are wondering what is going on. Well, keep wondering, until the truth makes everything clear. This man is Pyramus, if you want to know. This beautiful lady is definitely Thisbe. This man with the limestone and cement is portraying Wall, that horrible wall that kept these lovers apart. They are content to whisper through Wall's little hole, the poor souls, and no one should be surprised. This man, with his lantern, dog, and thornbush, portrays Moonshine, because, if you want to know, the lovers were not ashamed to meet each other by moonshine at Ninus's tomb in order to carry on their courtship. This grisly beast, which is called "Lion," scared away, or rather frightened, the faithful Thisbe when she arrived at the meeting place at night. As she ran away from him, she dropped her cloak, which the horrible Lion stained with his bloody mouth. Soon Pyramus comes along, a tall and handsome young man, and finds his faithful Thisbe's cloak to be dead. At this point, he takes his sword, his bloody blameful blade, and bravely breaks open his boiling bloody breast. And Thisbe, hiding in the shade of the mulberry bushes, took his dagger and killed herself. For the rest of the story, let Lion, Moonshine, Wall, and the two lovers talk more about it, since they're standing here.

THESEUS
I wonder if the lion be to speak.

DEMETRIUS
No wonder, my lord. One lion may when many asses do.

Exeunt PROLOGUE, PYRAMUS, THISBE,
LION, *and* MOONSHINE

WALL
(*played by* SNOUT) In this same interlude it doth befall
That I, one Snout by name, present a wall.
155   And such a wall, as I would have you think,
That had in it a crannied hole, or chink,
Through which the lovers, Pyramus and Thisbe,
Did whisper often very secretly.
This loam, this roughcast, and this stone doth show
160   That I am that same wall. The truth is so.
And this the cranny is, right and sinister,
Through which the fearful lovers are to whisper.

THESEUS
Would you desire lime and hair to speak better?

DEMETRIUS
It is the wittiest partition that ever I heard discourse,
165   my lord.

Enter PYRAMUS

THESEUS
Pyramus draws near the wall. Silence!

PYRAMUS
(*played by* BOTTOM)
O grim-looked night! O night with hue so black!
O night, which ever art when day is not!
O night, O night! Alack, alack, alack,

THESEUS

I wonder if the lion's going to talk.

DEMETRIUS

It wouldn't surprise me, my lord. If these asses can speak, a lion should be able to.

PROLOGUE, THISBE, LION, and MOONSHINE exit.

WALL

(played by SNOUT) At this point I, Snout, play a wall. But not just any wall. I want you to understand that I'm pretending to be a kind of wall that has a little hole in it. The lovers Pyramus and Thisbe often whispered very secretly through that hole. This clay, this cement, and this stone that I'm carrying around show that I'm that wall. It's the truth. And this is the crack, right side and left side *(points with two fingers)*, through which the frightened lovers will be whispering.

THESEUS

Can you imagine cement and stone talking better?

DEMETRIUS

It's the smartest partition I've ever heard speak, my lord.

PYRAMUS enters.

THESEUS

Pyramus is coming up to the wall. Be quiet!

PYRAMUS

(played by BOTTOM) Oh, grim-looking night! Oh, night that is so black in color! Oh night, which is always there when it is not day! Oh night! Oh night! So sad, sad, sad, I'm afraid my Thisbe has forgotten her promise!—And you, oh Wall, oh sweet, oh lovely

ACT FIVE

170   I fear my Thisbe's promise is forgot!—
         And thou, O Wall, O sweet, O lovely Wall,
         That stand'st between her father's ground and mine.
         Thou Wall, O Wall, O sweet and lovely Wall,
         Show me thy chink to blink through with mine eyne!

         WALL *holds up fingers as chink*

175   Thanks, courteous Wall. Jove shield thee well for this!
         But what see I? No Thisbe do I see.
         O wicked Wall through whom I see no bliss!
         Cursed be thy stones for thus deceiving me!

         THESEUS
         The wall, methinks, being sensible, should curse again.

         BOTTOM
180   *(out of character)* No, in truth, sir, he should not.
         "Deceiving me" is Thisbe's cue. She is to enter now and I
         am to spy her through the wall. You shall see, it will fall pat
         as I told you. Yonder she comes.

         Enter THISBE

         THISBE
         (played by FLUTE*)*
         O Wall, full often hast thou heard my moans,
185   For parting my fair Pyramus and me!
         My cherry lips have often kissed thy stones,
         Thy stones with lime and hair knit up in thee.

         PYRAMUS
         I see a voice. Now will I to the chink,
         To spy an I can hear my Thisbe's face. Thisbe?

         THISBE
190   My love thou art, my love, I think.

Wall, you stand between her father's property and mine, you Wall, oh Wall, oh sweet and lovely Wall. Show me your hole to stick my eye up against! *(WALL holds up two fingers)* Thank you, you're such a polite wall. God bless you for doing this. But what's this I see? I don't see any Thisbe. Oh wicked wall, through which I don't see any happiness! Damn your stones for disappointing me like this!

THESEUS

Since the wall is conscious, it should curse back at him.

BOTTOM

(out of character) No, actually, sir, he shouldn't say anything. It's not his turn, it's Thisbe's. "Disappointing me like this" is Thisbe's cue. She's supposed to enter now, and I'll see her through the wall. You'll see, it'll happen exactly like I say. Here she comes.

THISBE *enters.*

THISBE

(played by FLUTE) Oh wall, you've often heard me moaning because you keep me separated from my handsome Pyramus! My cherry lips have often kissed your bricks, which are stuck together with cement.

PYRAMUS

I see a voice! I'll go to the hole to see if I can hear my Thisbe's face. Thisbe?

THISBE

You are my love, my love, I think.

ACT FIVE

PYRAMUS
Think what thou wilt, I am thy lover's grace.
And like Limander am I trusty still.

THISBE
And I like Helen, till the Fates me kill.

PYRAMUS
Not Shafalus to Procrus was so true.

THISBE
195 As Shafalus to Procrus, I to you.

PYRAMUS
Oh, kiss me through the hole of this vile wall!

THISBE
I kiss the wall's hole, not your lips at all.

PYRAMUS
Wilt thou at Ninny's tomb meet me straightway?

THISBE
Tide life, tide death, I come without delay.

Exeunt PYRAMUS *and* THISBE

WALL
200 Thus have I, Wall, my part dischargèd so.
And, being done, thus Wall away doth go.

Exit WALL

PYRAMUS

I'm your love, no matter what you think. And I'm still faithful to you, just like the famous Limander.

Bottom means the mythical Greek hero Leander, who loved Hero.

THISBE

And I'll be as faithful to you as Helen of Troy, until the day I die.

This is funny not only because Leander loved Hero rather than Helen, but also because Helen was famous for being unfaithful to her husband.

PYRAMUS

Not even Shafalus was as faithful to his lover Procrus as I am to you.

THISBE

Me too, I'm as faithful as Shafalus to Procrus.

They mean to say Cephalus and Procris, two steadfast lovers in Greek mythology.

PYRAMUS

Oh, kiss me through the hole in this nasty wall.

THISBE

But I'm only kissing the wall's hole, not your lips at all.

PYRAMUS

Will you meet me right away at Ninny's grave?

THISBE

Neither death nor life will stop me from coming.

PYRAMUS *and* THISBE *exit.*

WALL

I, Wall, have done my part. Now that I'm done, Wall can go away.

WALL *exits.*

THESEUS
Now is the mural down between the two neighbors.

DEMETRIUS
No remedy, my lord, when walls are so willful to hear without warning.

HIPPOLYTA
205   This is the silliest stuff that ever I heard.

THESEUS
The best in this kind are but shadows, and the worst are no worse if imagination amend them.

HIPPOLYTA
It must be your imagination then, and not theirs.

THESEUS
If we imagine no worse of them than they of themselves,
210   they may pass for excellent men. Here come two noble beasts in, a man and a lion.

Enter LION *and* MOONSHINE

LION
(played by SNUG*)*
You, ladies, you whose gentle hearts do fear
The smallest monstrous mouse that creeps on floor,
May now perchance both quake and tremble here,
215   When lion rough in wildest rage doth roar.
Then know that I, as Snug the joiner, am
A lion fell, nor else no lion's dam.
For if I should as lion come in strife
Into this place, 'twere pity on my life.

THESEUS
220   A very gentle beast, of a good conscience.

DEMETRIUS
The very best at a beast, my lord, that e'er I saw.

THESEUS

The lovers should've waited around a little longer—
the wall between them is down now.

DEMETRIUS

What can you do? That's what happens with talking
walls.

HIPPOLYTA

This is the silliest thing I've ever seen.

THESEUS

The best plays are still only illusions, and the worst
are just as good, if you just use your imagination to fill
them in.

HIPPOLYTA

In that case it's your imagination that's interesting,
not the play.

THESEUS

If we imagine these guys as they imagine themselves,
then they're first-class actors. Look, here come two
noble animals, a man and a lion.

LION *and* MOONSHINE *enter.*

LION

(played by SNUG*)* You, ladies, whose gentle hearts make
you afraid of the smallest monstrous mouse that
crawls around on the floor, might quake and tremble
now when the wild lion roars in his most violent rage.
You should know that I, Snug the carpenter, am not a
fierce lion or a lioness, because if I were a lion and I
showed up here to cause trouble, I'd be taking my life
in my hands.

THESEUS

Ah, it's a sensitive animal, with a good conscience.

DEMETRIUS

He's the best actor I've ever seen play a lion.

LYSANDER
This lion is a very fox, for his valor.

THESEUS
True. And a goose for his discretion.

DEMETRIUS
Not so, my lord. For his valor cannot carry his discretion,
225   and the fox carries the goose.

THESEUS
His discretion, I am sure, cannot carry his valor, for the
goose carries not the fox. It is well. Leave it to his discretion,
and let us listen to the moon.

MOONSHINE
(played by **STARVELING***)*
This lanthorn doth the hornèd moon present—

DEMETRIUS
230   He should have worn the horns on his head.

THESEUS
He is no crescent, and his horns are invisible within the
circumference.

MOONSHINE
This lanthorn doth the hornèd moon present.
Myself the man i' th' moon do seem to be—

THESEUS
235   This is the greatest error of all the rest. The man should be
put into the lanthorn. How is it else the "man i' th' moon"?

DEMETRIUS
He dares not come there for the candle. For you see, it is
already in snuff.

HIPPOLYTA
I am aweary of this moon. Would he would change!

THESEUS
240   It appears by his small light of discretion, that he is in the
wane. But yet, in courtesy, in all reason, we must stay the
time.

LYSANDER

He's as brave as a fox.

THESEUS

True. And as wise as a goose.

DEMETRIUS

Oh, that's not true, my lord. He's not brave enough to be wise.

THESEUS

He's not wise enough to be brave. Anyway, he is what he is. Let's listen to the moon.

MOONSHINE

This lantern represents the horned moon—

horned moon = crescent moon

DEMETRIUS

He should have worn the horns on his head.

Cuckolds (husbands whose wives cheat on them) were imagined as having horns.

THESEUS

He's not a crescent moon, so his horns must be invisible inside the circle.

MOONSHINE

This lantern represents the moon. I myself am playing the man in the moon—

THESEUS

Well then, that's the biggest mistake of all. The man should be inside the lantern. How else is he the "man in the moon"?

DEMETRIUS

He can't go in there because of the candle. It's too hot.

HIPPOLYTA

I'm tired of this moon. I wish he'd wax or wane off the stage.

THESEUS

It seems like he's waning, but out of politeness we'll have to wait and see.

ACT FIVE

LYSANDER
Proceed, Moon.

MOONSHINE
All that I have to say is to tell you that the lanthorn is the
245   moon; I, the man in the moon; this thornbush, my
thornbush; and this dog, my dog.

DEMETRIUS
Why, all these should be in the lanthorn, for all these are in
the moon.—But silence! Here comes Thisbe.

Enter THISBE

THISBE
This is old Ninny's tomb. Where is my love?

LION
250   *(roaring)* Oh!

THISBE *runs off, dropping her mantle*

DEMETRIUS
Well roared, Lion!

THESEUS
Well run, Thisbe!

HIPPOLYTA
Well shone, Moon!—Truly, the moon shines with a good
grace.

LION *bloodies* THISBE*'s mantle*

THESEUS
255   Well moused, Lion!

Enter PYRAMUS

LYSANDER

Go ahead, Moon.

MOONSHINE

All I wanted to tell you is that the lantern is the moon, I'm the man in the moon, this thornbush is my thornbush, and this dog is my dog.

DEMETRIUS

Well, all of these should be in the lantern, because they're all in the moon. But be quiet, here comes Thisbe.

THISBE *enters.*

THISBE

This is old Ninny's tomb. But where is my love?

LION

(roaring) Hey!

THISBE *runs off, dropping her cloak.*

DEMETRIUS

Good roaring, Lion!

THESEUS

Good running, Thisbe!

HIPPOLYTA

Good shining, Moon!—Really, the Moon shines very well.

LION *shakes* THISBE*'s cloak around and stains it with blood.*

THESEUS

That's good, Lion! Shake it around like a cat with a mouse.

PYRAMUS *enters.*

DEMETRIUS
And then came Pyramus.

Exit LION

LYSANDER
And so the lion vanished.

PYRAMUS
Sweet Moon, I thank thee for thy sunny beams.
I thank thee, Moon, for shining now so bright.
260   For by thy gracious, golden, glittering gleams,
I trust to take of truest Thisbe sight.—
But stay, O spite!
But mark, poor knight,
What dreadful dole is here!
265   Eyes, do you see?
How can it be?
O dainty duck! O dear!
Thy mantle good,
What, stained with blood?
270   Approach, ye Furies fell!
O Fates, come, come,
Cut thread and thrum.
Quail, crush, conclude, and quell!

THESEUS
This passion and the death of a dear friend would go near to
275   make a man look sad.

HIPPOLYTA
Beshrew my heart, but I pity the man.

PYRAMUS
O wherefore, Nature, didst thou lions frame?
Since lion vile hath here deflowered my dear,
Which is—no, no—which was the fairest dame
280   That lived, that loved, that liked, that looked with cheer.
Come, tears, confound!
Out, sword, and wound!
The pap of Pyramus—

DEMETRIUS

And then Pyramus showed up.

LION *exits.*

LYSANDER

So the lion disappeared.

PYRAMUS

Sweet Moon, I thank you for your sunny beams. I thank you, Moon, for shining now so bright, because by the light of your gracious, golden, glittering gleams, I hope to be able to see my faithful Thisbe.— But wait. Oh no! But, look, poor me, what a terrible tragedy is here! Eyes, do you see? How can it be? Oh, dainty duck! Oh, dear! Your cloak so good, what, stained with blood? Come, terrible Furies, and punish whoever has hurt her! Oh, Fate, come and cut the thread of my life. Conquer, crush, conclude, and kill!

THESEUS

You could get sad watching this actor's passionate lament—if one of your good friends happened to die right at the same time.

HIPPOLYTA

Damned if I don't feel sorry for him.

PYRAMUS

Oh, Mother Nature, why did you create lions? A mean and awful lion has deflowered my darling, who is—no, no, who was the most beautiful lady who ever lived, or loved, or liked, or looked. Come on, tears, pour over me! Come on out, sword, and wound Pyra-

Bottom means "devoured," since "deflowered" would mean that the lion had taken Thisbe's virginity.

Ay, that left pap
285   Where heart doth hop. *(stabs himself)*

Thus die I, thus, thus, thus.
Now am I dead.
Now am I fled.
My soul is in the sky.
290   Tongue, lose thy light.
Moon, take thy flight.

Exit MOONSHINE

Now die, die, die, die, die.
(dies)

DEMETRIUS
No die, but an ace for him, for he is but one.

LYSANDER
Less than an ace, man. For he is dead. He is nothing.

THESEUS
295   With the help of a surgeon he might yet recover and prove
an ass.

HIPPOLYTA
How chance Moonshine is gone before Thisbe comes back
and finds her lover?

THESEUS
She will find him by starlight. Here she comes, and her
300   passion ends the play.

Enter THISBE

HIPPOLYTA
Methinks she should not use a long one for such a Pyramus.
I hope she will be brief.

DEMETRIUS
A mote will turn the balance, which Pyramus, which
Thisbe, is the better. He for a man, God warrant us, she for
305   a woman, God bless us.

mus in the chest—yes, right here on the left side where his heart is. *(PYRAMUS stabs himself)*

And so I'm dying. Here I go, here I go. Okay, now I'm dead. My soul has fled to the sky. My tongue shall see no more, It's time for the moon to go away.

MOONSHINE exits.

Now die, die, die, die, die. *(PYRAMUS dies)*

DEMETRIUS

Is someone throwing dice? I guess it's "die," not dice, since there's only one of him.

LYSANDER

Actually he's a die with no dots, since he's nothing— he's dead.

THESEUS

With a doctor's help he might recover and become an ass again.

HIPPOLYTA

If Moonshine's gone before Thisbe comes back, how will she be able to see in the dark to find her lover dead?

THESEUS

She'll see him by starlight. Here she comes. Her moaning and groaning will end the play.

THISBE enters.

HIPPOLYTA

I don't think a ridiculous Pyramus like that one deserves much moaning. I hope she keeps it short.

DEMETRIUS

I can't decide whether Pyramus or Thisbe is better. God help us if he's a better man. But God help us if she's a better woman.

ACT FIVE

LYSANDER
    She hath spied him already with those sweet eyes.

DEMETRIUS
    And thus she means, videlicet—

THISBE
    Asleep, my love?
    What, dead, my dove?
310   O Pyramus, arise!
    Speak, speak. Quite dumb?
    Dead, dead? A tomb
    Must cover thy sweet eyes.
    These lily lips,
315   This cherry nose,
    These yellow cowslip cheeks
    Are gone, are gone.
    Lovers, make moan.
    His eyes were green as leeks.
320   O Sisters three,
    Come, come to me
    With hands as pale as milk.
    Lay them in gore,
    Since you have shore
325   With shears his thread of silk.
    Tongue, not a word.
    Come, trusty sword.
    Come, blade, my breast imbrue. *(stabs herself)*
    And, farewell, friends.
330   Thus Thisbe ends.
    Adieu, adieu, adieu.
    (dies)

THESEUS
    Moonshine and Lion are left to bury the dead.

DEMETRIUS
    Ay, and Wall too.

LYSANDER

Look, she's spotted him with those sweet eyes of hers.

DEMETRIUS

And now she'll start moaning, of course—

THISBE

Are you asleep, my love? What, are you dead, my dove? Oh, Pyramus, get up! Speak, speak. Can't you talk? Dead, dead? The dirt of a grave must cover your sweet eyes! Your lily-white lips, your cherry-red nose, and your buttercup-yellow cheeks are gone, gone forever. Lovers, moan and weep. His eyes were as green as leeks. Oh, Fate, come, come to me, with hands as pale as milk. Soak your hands in blood and gore, since you have cut the thread of his life with scissors. Tongue, do not speak. Come, trusty sword. Come, blade, drench my breast with blood. *(she stabs herself)* Goodbye, friends! This is how Thisbe comes to an end. Goodbye, goodbye, goodbye. (THISBE *dies)*

THESEUS

Moonshine and Lion are left to bury the dead.

DEMETRIUS

Yes, and Wall too.

BOTTOM

(out of character) No, assure you. The wall is down that

335   parted their fathers. Will it please you to see the epilogue,

or to hear a Bergomask dance between two of our company?

THESEUS

No epilogue, I pray you, for your play needs no excuse. Never

excuse—for when the players are all dead, there needs none

to be blamed. Marry, if he that writ it had played Pyramus

335   and hanged himself in Thisbe's garter, it would have been a

fine tragedy. And so it is, truly, and very notably discharged.

But come, your Bergomask. Let your epilogue alone.

Bergomask dance

                                      Exeunt BOTTOM *and* FLUTE

The iron tongue of midnight hath told twelve.

Lovers, to bed. 'Tis almost fairy time.

345   I fear we shall outsleep the coming morn

As much as we this night have overwatched.

This palpable-gross play hath well beguiled

The heavy gait of night. Sweet friends, to bed.

A fortnight hold we this solemnity,

350   In nightly revels and new jollity.

                                               Exeunt

Enter ROBIN

ROBIN

                     Now the hungry lion roars

                     And the wolf behowls the moon,

                     Whilst the heavy ploughman snores,

                     All with weary task fordone.

355   Now the wasted brands do glow,

                     Whilst the screech-owl, screeching loud,

                     Puts the wretch that lies in woe

                     In remembrance of a shroud.

                     Now it is the time of night

360   That the graves all gaping wide,

BOTTOM

(out of character) No, I assure you. The wall that kept their fathers apart has been taken down. Would you like to see the epilogue or hear a country dance between two of us?

THESEUS

No epilogue, please. Your play doesn't need to be excused afterward with an epilogue. Never apologize—when the actors are all dead, no one can be blamed. As a matter of fact, if the playwright had played Pyramus and hanged himself with Thisbe's belt, it would have been a very good tragedy. It's a good tragedy, very well done. But come on, let's see you do your dance. Forget your epilogue.

The actors dance, and BOTTOM *and* FLUTE *exit.*

The clock has chimed midnight. Lovers, it's time to go to bed. It's almost fairy time. I'm afraid we're going to oversleep in the morning as late as we've stayed up tonight. This blatantly stupid play helped us kill the time until bed. Dear friends, let's go to bed. We'll continue this celebration for two weeks, with nightly parties and new fun.

They all exit.

ROBIN *enters.*

ROBIN

Now the hungry lion roars and the wolf howls at the moon. The farmer snores, exhausted from his work. The charred logs glow in the fireplace, and the owl's hoot makes the sick man think about his own death. Now is the time of night when graves open wide and release spirits to glide over the graveyard paths. And we fairies, who run away from the sun just like the

ACT FIVE

Every one lets forth his sprite,
In the churchway paths to glide.
And we fairies, that do run
By the triple Hecate's team
365   From the presence of the sun,
Following darkness like a dream,
Now are frolic. Not a mouse
Shall disturb this hallowed house.
I am sent with broom before
370   To sweep the dust behind the door.

Enter OBERON *and* TITANIA, *King and Queen of Fairies, with all their train*

OBERON
Through the house give glimmering light,
By the dead and drowsy fire.
Every elf and fairy sprite
Hop as light as bird from brier.
375   And this ditty, after me,
Sing and dance it trippingly.

TITANIA
First, rehearse your song by rote,
To each word a warbling note.
Hand in hand with fairy grace
380   Will we sing and bless this place.

OBERON, TITANIA, *and the* FAIRIES *sing and dance*

OBERON
(*sings*)
Now until the break of day,
Through this house each fairy stray.
To the best bride bed will we,
Which by us shall blessèd be.
385   *And the issue there create*
Ever shall be fortunate.
So shall all the couples three

goddess of the night, following darkness like a dream, are getting antsy. But I'm here to make sure that not even a mouse disturbs this blessed house. I've been sent to clean house a bit before the fairies come.

OBERON and TITANIA enter with their servants and followers.

OBERON

Let the dying fire shine a glimmering light throughout the house. I want every elf and fairy to hop lightly, like a bird on a twig, and to sing and dance this song along with me.

TITANIA

First rehearse your song from memory, and make sure each note is pretty. We'll all join hands and sing, and bless this place with our fairy grace.

OBERON and TITANIA lead the FAIRIES in song and dance.

OBERON

(singing)
> Now, until morning, each fairy should walk through this house. Titania and I will go to the royal marriage bed to bless it, and the children conceived in that bed will always have good luck. Each of the three couples will always be faithful and in love, and their children will have no

Ever true in loving be.
And the blots of Nature's hand
390 *Shall not in their issue stand.*
Never mole, harelip, nor scar,
Nor mark prodigious, such as are
Despisèd in nativity,
Shall upon their children be.
395 *With this field dew consecrate,*
Every fairy take his gait.
And each several chamber bless
Through this palace with sweet peace.
And the owner of it blessed
400 *Ever shall in safety rest.*
Trip away. Make no stay.
Meet me all by break of day.

Exeunt all but ROBIN

ROBIN

If we shadows have offended,
Think but this, and all is mended—
405 That you have but slumbered here
While these visions did appear.
And this weak and idle theme,
No more yielding but a dream,
Gentles, do not reprehend.
410 If you pardon, we will mend.
And, as I am an honest Puck,
If we have unearnèd luck
Now to 'scape the serpent's tongue,
We will make amends ere long.
415 Else the Puck a liar call.
So good night unto you all.
Give me your hands if we be friends,
And Robin shall restore amends.

Exit

deformities. They won't have moles, or harelips, or scars, or abnormal markings, or anything else that might alarm someone if their baby was born with it. Use this blessed dew from the fields to bless each room in the palace with sweet peace. And the blessed owner will always be safe. Run along. Don't stay long. Meet me at dawn.

They all exit except for ROBIN.

ROBIN

If we actors have offended you, just think of it this way and everything will be all right—you were asleep when you saw these visions, and this silly and pathetic story was no more real than a dream. Ladies and gentlemen, don't get upset with me. If you forgive us, we'll make everything all right. I'm an honest Puck, and I swear that if we're lucky enough not to get hissed at, we'll make it up to you soon. If not, then I'm a liar. So good night to everyone. Give me some applause, if we're friends, and Robin will make everything up to you.

He exits.

NOTES

PART III

STUDY
GUIDE

6

THEMATIC QUESTIONS

1. Discuss the role of the play-within-a-play in Act V of *A Midsummer Night's Dream*. Does the Pyramus and Thisbe story have any relevance to the main story, or is it simply a comical interlude? What effect does the craftsmen's production of their play have on the tone of *A Midsummer Night's Dream* as a whole?

The story of Pyramus and Thisbe offers a very subtle return to a couple of the main elements of *A Midsummer Night's Dream*: lovers caught up in misunderstanding and sorrow enhanced by the darkness of night. Like the main story of the outer play, the inner play consists of a tragic premise made comical by the actors. The craftsmen's unintentionally goofy portrayal of the woe of Pyramus and Thisbe makes the melodramatic romantic entanglements of the young Athenian lovers seem even more comical.

However, it is important to recognize as well that the inherent structure of a play-within-a-play allows Shakespeare to show off his talent by inserting a gem of pure comedy. The conflicts have been resolved and a happy ending procured for all; the performance, thus, has no impact on the plot. Rather, the craftsmen's hilarious bungling of the heavy tragedy allows the audience, and the melodramatic Athenian lovers, to laugh and take delight in the spectacle of the play.

2. How does the play's broad frame of reference heighten its use of contrast as an atmospheric device? More generally, how does Shakespeare use contrasting tones and characters in the play?

That Shakespeare takes his characters from vastly different sources (e.g., the bumbling, rough craftsmen and the delicate, fanciful fairies) contributes to the imaginative scope and pervasive absurdity of *A Midsummer Night's Dream*. Shakespeare combines the contrasting elements of the play in startling and grotesque ways, as in the royal Titania's love for the ass-headed Bottom. He thus creates the sense that the normal rules and operations of reality have been suspended: if the magical Titania can fall in love with the ludicrous Bottom, anything can happen. The play's extraordinarily varied frame of reference, which includes elements of Greek mythology (Theseus and Hippolyta), aspects of the contemporary London theatrical tradition (males playing females in the craftsmen's play), characters of Babylonian origin (Pyramus and Thisbe) and from English fairy lore (Puck), and classical literary analogues (Titania and Oberon), adds to the surreal quality of the play by juxtaposing elements that clash stylistically.

3. How is *A Midsummer Night's Dream* structured? Is there anything unusual in its treatment of the five-act dramatic form?

A Midsummer Night's Dream fits into four acts all of the material that would normally occupy a five-act play; the main story, climax, and even a period of falling action are capped by a happy turn of events that would seem to mark the play's end. It is somewhat strange, then, that Shakespeare includes a fifth act. Since he has already resolved the tensions of the main plot, he treats Act V as a joyful comic epilogue. Except for a short closing scene, the act is committed wholly to the craftsmen's performance of Pyramus and Thisbe. In wrapping up the conflict before the last act, Shakespeare affords himself the opportunity to give the audience one act of pure, uncomplicated comedy. He offers a play-within-a-play whose comical rendition caps the cheerful mood of the Athenians watching.

CHAPTER

7

KEY QUESTIONS
AND ANSWERS

1. What is Egeus so upset about in the play's first scene?

Egeus is upset because his daughter, Hermia, has challenged his authority. When Egeus approaches Theseus at the beginning of Act I, he has just learned that Hermia rejected his preferred suitor, Demetrius. Presumably Egeus prefers Demetrius for reasons related to wealth and status. But, as Lysander points out, he possesses just as much wealth and status as his rival. What's more, he also possesses Hermia's heart. "Why," he asks, "should not I then prosecute my right?" Yet Lysander's rational and compelling argument does little to calm Egeus's fury. Possibly Egeus's anger derives less from Hermia's preference for one lover over another, and more from her public rejection of his authority. By rejecting Egeus's authority, Hermia spurns the patriarchal laws of Athenian society. Theseus indicates as much when he reminds her, "To you your father should be as a god" (I.i.).

2. Why do Peter Quince and his fellow craftsmen want to perform a play for Theseus and Hippolyta's wedding?

The band of craftsmen want to perform a play at the Athenian nobles' wedding because they hope their performance will win them a cash prize. However, their motivation doesn't become clear until Act IV. The group returns to Athens

STUDY GUIDE

without Bottom, fearing that they've lost their chances at performing. Snug laments, "If our sport had gone forward, we had all been made men" (IV.ii.). Flute says that Bottom has "lost sixpence a day." Apparently, the craftsmen believe that their performance would have won them each a fortune, and Bottom in particular would have performed so well that Theseus would have awarded him a generous pension of sixpence a day. This economic motivation for performing underscores the enormous class difference between the craftsmen and the nobles. Class difference also contributes to the subtle irony of Peter Quince's prologue, which he recites with incorrect punctuation so that in Act V he ends up saying the opposite of what he means: "If we offend, it is with our good will" (V.i.). Although humorous, Quince's mistake quietly suggests the tension between socioeconomic classes.

3. Why does Oberon order Puck to fetch the smagic flower?

Oberon orders Puck to fetch the magic flower to get back at Titania. Oberon and Titania are estranged from one another for a couple of reasons. First, the fairy king and queen are both jealous of each other's attraction to their counterparts in the human realm. Just as Oberon is attracted to Hippolyta, so Titania is attracted to Theseus, and in Act II the couple confronts each other with their jealous suspicions. But Oberon and Titania are also estranged due to a dispute about a human Indian child who was stolen by one of Titania's worshippers and replaced with a fairy changeling. This Indian child has been left in Titania's care, and she refuses Oberon when he asks to have the child as his "henchman." Titania's refusal is the last straw for Oberon, who in his anger makes the following pledge: "Thou shalt not from this grove / Till I torment thee for this injury" (II.i.). After making this vow Oberon turns to Puck and instructs him to fetch a magic flower whose juice "Will make or man or woman madly dote / Upon the next live creature that it sees" (II.i.).

4. Why does Puck delight in causing chaos and confusion?

Puck delights in causing chaos and confusion because he's a fairy, and according to tradition causing mischief is exactly what fairies do. Puck in particular has achieved fame for his many mischievous exploits. The audience gets a sense for Puck's legendary status in Act II, when an unnamed fairy recognizes him and talks excitedly about some of his most well-known tricks. Puck goes on to describe some of the other great tricks he's played on unsuspecting humans. Although Puck never explicitly describes why chaos delights him so much, he does offer a hint when he exclaims, "And those things do best please me / That befall preposterously" (III.ii.). Puck's use of the word "preposterously" is significant here. This word derives from two Latin words, one that means "in front of" (prae) and one that means "behind" (posterus). Preposterous would then mean something like "with the behind in front." In other words, Puck loves to flip things around and turn them on their head. Although Puck's antics may cause pain or frustration for his human targets, he and his fellow fairies take great delight in causing trouble.

5. What causes the animosity between Hermia and Helena?

Hermia and Helena have enjoyed a close friendship since they were young, but recently their friendship has come under strain due to their entanglement in a knot of desire and jealousy. Before the play begins, Helena and Demetrius were in a loving relationship, as were Hermia and Lysander. Everything changed, however, when Demetrius turned his amorous gaze from Helena in order to pursue Hermia. Suddenly, Hermia had two suitors, and Helena had none. Helena is left feeling cast aside and unappealing. At the beginning of the play, she makes a big deal about her jealousy of Hermia, saying, "Your eyes are lodestars, and your tongue's sweet air / More tunable than lark to shepherd's ear" (I.i.). What starts out as mere jealousy becomes full-blown animosity by Act III. Lysander, charmed by fairy magic, abandons Hermia and pursues Helena instead. This reversal induces Hermia to rage and causes great torment for Helena. The friends' heightened emotions cause them to argue spitefully and call each other cruel names. Although fairy mischief amplifies the animosity between Hermia and Helena, it's important to emphasize that this animosity originated with Demetrius. It is the inconstant desire of a single man that drives a wedge between these women.

8

THEMES, MOTIFS,
AND SYMBOLS

Themes

Themes are the fundamental and often universal ideas explored in a literary work.

LOVE'S DIFFICULTY

"The course of true love never did run smooth," comments Lysander, articulating one of *A Midsummer Night's Dream's* most important themes—that of the difficulty of love (I.i.). Though most of the conflict in the play stems from the troubles of romance, and though the play involves a number of romantic elements, it is not truly a love story; it distances the audience from the emotions of the characters in order to poke fun at the torments and afflictions that those in love suffer. The tone of the play is so lighthearted that the audience never doubts that things will end happily, and it is therefore free to enjoy the comedy without being caught up in the tension of an uncertain outcome.

The theme of love's difficulty is often explored through the motif of love out of balance—that is, romantic situations in which a disparity or inequality interferes with the harmony of a relationship. The prime instance of this imbalance is the asymmetrical love among the four young Athenians: Hermia loves Lysander, Lysander loves Hermia, Helena loves Demetrius, and Demetrius loves Hermia instead of Helena—a simple numeric imbalance in which two men love the same woman, leaving one woman with too many suitors and one with too few. The play has strong potential for a traditional outcome, and the plot is in many ways based on a quest for internal balance; that is, when the lovers' tangle resolves itself into symmetrical pairings, the traditional happy ending will have been achieved. Somewhat similarly, in the relationship between Titania and Oberon, an imbalance arises out of the fact that Oberon's coveting of Titania's Indian boy outweighs his love for her. Later, Titania's passion for the ass-headed Bottom represents an imbalance of appearance and nature: Titania is beautiful and graceful, while Bottom is clumsy and grotesque.

MAGIC

The fairies' magic, which brings about many of the most bizarre and hilarious situations in the play, is another element central to the fantastic atmosphere of *A Midsummer Night's Dream*. Shakespeare uses magic both to embody the almost supernatural power of love (symbolized by the love potion) and to create a surreal world. Although the misuse of magic causes chaos, as when Puck mistakenly applies the love potion to Lysander's eyelids, magic ultimately resolves the play's tensions by restoring love to balance among the quartet of Athenian youths. Additionally, the ease with which Puck uses magic to his own ends, as when he reshapes Bottom's head into that of an ass and recreates the voices of Lysander and Demetrius, stands in contrast to the laboriousness and gracelessness of the craftsmen's attempt to stage their play.

DREAMS

As the title suggests, dreams are an important theme in *A Midsummer Night's Dream*; they are linked to the bizarre, magical mishaps in the forest. Hippolyta's first words in the play evidence the prevalence of dreams ("Four days will quickly steep themselves in night. / Four nights will quickly dream away the time"), and various characters mention dreams throughout (I.i.). The theme of dreaming recurs predominantly when characters attempt to explain bizarre events in which these characters are involved: "I have had a dream—past the wit of man to say what dream it was. Man is but an ass if he go about to expound this dream," (IV.i.) Bottom says, unable to fathom the magical happenings that have affected him as anything but the result of slumber.

Shakespeare is also interested in the actual workings of dreams, in how events occur without explanation, time loses its normal sense of flow, and the impossible occurs as a matter of course; he seeks to recreate this environment in the play through the intervention of the fairies in the magical forest. At the end of the play, Puck extends the idea of dreams to the audience members themselves, saying that, if they have been offended by the play, they should remember it as nothing more than a dream. This sense of illusion and gauzy fragility is crucial to the atmosphere of *A Midsummer Night's Dream*, as it helps render the play a fantastical experience rather than a heavy drama.

MOTIFS

Motifs are recurring structures, contrasts, and literary devices that can help to develop and inform the text's major themes.

CONTRAST

The idea of contrast is the basic building block of *A Midsummer Night's Dream*. The entire play is constructed around groups of opposites and doubles. Nearly every characteristic presented in the play has an opposite: Helena is tall, Hermia is short; Puck plays pranks, Bottom is the victim of pranks; Titania is beautiful, Bottom is grotesque. Further, the three main groups of characters (who are developed from sources as varied as Greek mythology, English folklore, and classical literature) are designed to contrast powerfully with one another: the fairies are graceful and magical, while the craftsmen are clumsy and earthy; the craftsmen are merry, while the lovers are overly serious. Contrast serves as the defining visual characteristic of *A Midsummer Night's Dream*, with the play's most indelible image being that of the beautiful, delicate Titania weaving flowers into the hair of the ass-headed Bottom. It seems impossible to imagine two figures less compatible with each other. The juxtaposition of extraordinary differences is the most important characteristic of the play's surreal atmosphere and is thus perhaps the play's central motif; there is no scene in which extraordinary contrast is not present.

SYMBOLS

Symbols are objects, characters, figures, and colors used to represent abstract ideas or concepts.

THESEUS AND HIPPOLYTA

Theseus and Hippolyta bookend *A Midsummer Night's Dream*, appearing in the daylight at both the beginning and the end of the play's main action. They disappear, however, for the duration of the action, leaving in the middle of Act I, scene i, and not reappearing until Act IV, as the sun is coming up to end the magical night in the forest. Shakespeare uses Theseus and Hippolyta, the ruler of Athens and his warrior bride, to represent order and stability, to contrast with the uncertainty, instability, and darkness of most of the play. Whereas an important element of the dream realm is that one is not in control of one's environment, Theseus and Hippolyta are always entirely in control of theirs. Their reappearance in the daylight of Act IV to hear Theseus's hounds signifies the end of the dream state of the previous night and a return to rationality.

THE LOVE POTION

The love potion is made from the juice of a flower that was struck with one of Cupid's misfired arrows; it is used by the fairies to wreak romantic havoc throughout Acts II, III, and IV. Because the meddling fairies are careless with the love potion, the situation of the young Athenian lovers becomes increasingly chaotic and confusing (Demetrius and Lysander are magically compelled to transfer their love from Hermia to Helena), and Titania is hilariously humiliated (she is magically compelled to fall deeply in love with the ass-headed Bottom). The love potion thus becomes a symbol of the unreasoning, fickle, erratic, and undeniably powerful nature of love, which can lead to inexplicable and bizarre behavior and cannot be resisted.

THE CRAFTSMEN'S PLAY

The play-within-a-play that takes up most of Act V, scene i, is used to represent, in condensed form, many of the important ideas and themes of the main plot. Because the craftsmen are such bumbling actors, their performance satirizes the melodramatic Athenian lovers and gives the play a purely joyful, comedic ending. Pyramus and Thisbe face parental disapproval in the play-within-a-play, just as Hermia and Lysander do; the theme of romantic confusion enhanced by the darkness of night is rehashed, as Pyramus mistakenly believes that Thisbe has been killed by the lion, just as the Athenian lovers experience intense misery because of the mix-ups caused by the fairies' meddling. The craftsmen's play is, therefore, a kind of symbol for *A Midsummer Night's Dream* itself: a story involving powerful emotions that is made hilarious by its comical presentation.

NOTES

NOTES

9

QUOTES AND ANALYSIS
BY THEME

JEALOUSY

> For ere Demetrius looked on Hermia's eyne,
>
> He hailed down oaths that he was only mine;
>
> And when this hail some heat from Hermia felt,
>
> So he dissolved, and showers of oaths did melt.
>
> (I.i.)

After Hermia and Lysander depart Athens for the forest, Helena expresses her jealousy of the lovers' happiness and particularly of Hermia's beauty. These lines come late in Helena's speech, and they serve at once to reiterate her jealousy of Hermia and to demonstrate the pain she feels at having lost the affections of Demetrius, the man who had promised himself to her and whom she still loves. Helena's language is suggestive. Her mention of heat and melting invokes the heat of both attraction and anger, yet her emphasis on eyes and showers also conjures figurative tears of pain.

> How canst thou thus for shame, Titania,
>
> Glance at my credit with Hippolyta,
>
> Knowing I know thy love to Theseus?
>
> (II.i.)

Oberon speaks these words to Titania after she has just implied that he wastes his time writing pointless poems and chasing after women. In particular, she mentions Oberon's lust for Hippolyta, whom Titania refers to as "the bouncing Amazon, / Your buskined mistress and your warrior love" (II.i.). Titania clearly feels jealous, and Oberon's touchy response in these lines shows that he is equally jealous of Titania, who has a thing for Theseus. Despite the undertone of jealousy, Oberon's point here is that Titania has no right to dishonor him by complaining about his actions when she is guilty of the same.

MISCHIEF

> *Are not you he*
> *That frights the maidens of the villagery,*
> *Skim milk, and sometimes labor in the quern*
> *And bootless make the breathless housewife churn,*
> *And sometime make the drink to bear no barm,*
> *Mislead night-wanderers, laughing at their harm?*
> *(II.i.)*

An anonymous fairy speaks these lines upon recognizing the infamous Puck, a puckish spirit who is well known in English folklore for performing various pranks on unsuspecting villagers. The tone of the unnamed fairy approximates that of an adoring fan. The awe with which he lists Puck's most typical pranks suggests just how much delight the fairy realm takes in promoting mischief. Puck makes this point explicitly in Act III when he declares, "And those things do best please me / That befall preposterously" (III.ii.).

> *What thou see'st when thou dost wake,*
> *Do it for thy true love take.*
> *Love and languish for his sake.*
> *Be it ounce or cat or bear,*
> *Pard or boar with bristled hair,*
> *In thy eye that shall appear*
> *When thou wakest, it is thy dear.*
> *Wake when some vile thing is near.*
> *(II.ii.)*

This is the spell Oberon utters while squeezing the liquid from an enchanted flower onto Titania's eyelids. Two things are worth noting here. First, Oberon's verse is made up of rhyming couplets in iambic tetrameter. In *A Midsummer Night's Dream*, the fairies often speak in this meter rather than the more usual iambic pentameter of the Athenian nobles. Thus the very meter of the language is associated in this play with mischief. Second, this particular enchantment stands as the play's primary act of mischief, which comically amplifies the discord among the play's lovers in anticipation of eventual resolution.

TRANSFORMATION

> *Why are you grown so rude? What change is this,*
>
> *Sweet love?*
>
> *(III.ii.)*

After Hermia wakes from her sleep to find Lysander gone, she tracks him down, only to be met with harsh insults from her betrothed. In these lines she asks Lysander what has turned his "sweet love" so bitter. Lysander's emotional transformation is, of course, the result of fairy mischief. His transformation is also metaphorically linked to the many other changes in affection that occur in the play, including Demetrius's shift from Helena to Hermia (and back to Helena) as well as Titania's shift from Bottom back to Oberon.

> *But all the story of the night told over,*
>
> *And all their minds transfigured so together,*
>
> *More witnesseth than fancy's images*
>
> *And grows to something of great constancy,*
>
> *But, howsoever, strange and admirable.*
>
> *(V.i.)*

As against Theseus's skepticism regarding the lovers' story of their night in the forest, Hippolyta utters these lines to express her belief in their story. She cites as evidence of the story's truthfulness the fact that "all their minds [have been] transfigured so together."

Hippolyta's use of the word "transfigured" is significant, since it indicates not just transformation, but transformation into something better, more elevated. Thus, the lovers' minds have all undergone a metamorphosis that has brought them to a higher, nobler place. The positive valence of this transformation clearly indicates that "something of great constancy" has transpired.

UNREASON

> *Methinks, mistress, you should have little reason for*
> *that [i.e., to love me]. And yet, to say the truth, reason*
> *and love keep little company together nowadays.*
> *(III.i)*

Bottom addresses these words to Titania after she swears her love to him. Though Bottom's head has been transformed into that of a donkey, he is not under the same love enchantment as Titania, and thus does not understand why she would have to love him. In spite of this, Bottom reasons that love and logic don't always go together. Amusingly, Titania responds to Bottom's illogic with an equally unreasonable conclusion: "Thou art as wise as thou art beautiful" (III.i.).

> *You speak not as you think. It cannot be.*
> *(III.ii.)*

Hermia speaks these words in response to Lysander, who has just asked her why she persists in following him: "Could not this make thee know / The hate I bear thee made me leave thee so?" (III.ii.). The sudden and complete reversal of Lysander's affections strikes Hermia as an impossible turn of events that cannot stand to reason. She conveys this feeling of unreason by pointing to the apparent contradiction between what Lysander says and what he thinks.

> *More strange than true. I never may believe*
> *These antique fables nor these fairy toys.*
> *Lovers and madmen have such seething brains,*

Such shaping fantasies, that apprehend

More than cool reason ever comprehends.

(V.i.)

After the lovers have returned to Athens and told the story of their wild night in the forest, Theseus expresses his skepticism. The strangeness of the events recounted strain his sense of reality, and so he attributes the lovers' belief in their own story to the idea that they, like madmen, suffer from "seething brains." This condition has diluted their mental faculties, allowing them to "apprehend / More than cool reason ever comprehends."

REVERSAL

Run when you will, the story shall be changed.

Apollo flies and Daphne holds the chase.

The dove pursues the griffin. The mild hind

Makes speed to catch the tiger—bootless speed,

When cowardice pursues and valor flies.

(II.i.)

As Helena follows Demetrius and continues to swear her love for him, he responds less than kindly, telling her, "I'll run from thee and hide me in the brakes" (II.i.). Helena retorts with these lines, observing how her pursuit of Demetrius reverses the usual state of affairs, in which the strong (man) pursues the weak (woman). Helena couches this idea of reversal in a reference to the myth of Apollo and Daphne. This myth involves the virgin nymph Daphne turning into a laurel tree to escape from the lustful god Apollo, who chases after her. Here, however, "Apollo flies and Daphne holds the chase."

You do advance your cunning more and more.

When truth kills truth, O devilish holy fray!

These vows are Hermia's. Will you give her o'er?

(III.ii.)

When the fairy enchantment shifts Lysander's affections from Hermia to Helena, Helena suspects that he, along with Demetrius, is trying to humiliate her with a prank. Lysander's love for Helena is not a strict reversal, since he did not previously hate her. Nevertheless, Helena understands this turn of events in terms of a negation in which "truth kills truth." Here, the truth of Lysander's vow to Helena negates his previous vow to Hermia. This negation has the effect of instigating conflict between Helena and Hermia, thereby reversing their relationship from friends to rivals.

> *I know you two are rival enemies.*
>
> *How comes this gentle concord in the world,*
>
> *That hatred is so far from jealousy*
>
> *To sleep by hate and fear no enmity?*
>
> *(IV.i.)*

Theseus addresses this question to Lysander and Demetrius, who have reconciled their differences. The reversal of rivalry into friendship clearly surprises Theseus, and the duke's surprise indicates his general failure of imagination. (This failure of imagination returns at the top of Act V, when Theseus refuses to believe the lovers' account of the previous night.) Despite Theseus's surprise at the reversal in Lysander and Demetrius's relationship, the entire play has been orchestrated to anticipate the eventuality of just such a reversal of discord into concord.

NOTES

NOTES

10

QUOTES AND ANALYSIS
BY CHARACTER

NICK BOTTOM

A very good piece of work, I assure you, and a merry.

(I.ii.)

Bottom announces his lack of self-awareness in this line from Act I. He is responding to Peter Quince, who has just told his actors the title of their play, *The Most Lamentable Comedy and Most Cruel Death of Pyramus and Thisbe*. Though partly framed as a comedy, it's difficult to imagine how something so "lamentable" and "cruel" could also be "merry." Like the rest of the craftsmen, Bottom clearly knows little about what separates comedy from tragedy.

Yet my chief humor is for a tyrant. I could play

Ercles rarely, or a part to tear a cat in to make all split.

(I.ii.)

In Act I Bottom declares his desire to play a tyrant, or perhaps hero like "Ercles," which is his humorous mispronunciation of Hercules. With these words, Bottom shows his lack of subtlety as a performer, as well as his penchant for the melodramatic. Bottom's words also reference a medieval tradition in which artisans used to perform bombastic plays on Christian feast days.

Some man or other must present Wall. And let him

> *have some plaster, or some loam, or some roughcast*
>
> *about him to signify wall.*
>
> *(III.i.)*

Bottom proposes a solution to the problem of how to have a wall without actually building one. The suggestion that someone should play the part of Wall may be amusing and completely absurd, but it also demonstrates a certain degree of ingenuity on Bottom's part. He may not be a genius of stagecraft, but in this and other examples he does work actively to resolve any issues that arise.

> *What do you see? You see an ass head of your own, do*
>
> *you?*
>
> *(III.i.)*

Bottom's companions react in fear after Puck has exchanged his human head for that of a donkey. In response to Snout's fearful exclamation, "thou art changed," Bottom retorts that Snout must actually be referring to his own sudden shift from calmness to agitation. When Bottom refers to Snout's sudden emotional change as "an ass head of your own," he means that Snout's behavior is idiotic. Yet the phrasing is unintentionally humorous, since in fact Bottom literally has the head of an ass.

PUCK GOODFELLOW

> *I am that merry wanderer of the night.*
>
> *I jest to Oberon and make him smile*
>
> *When I a fat and bean-fed horse beguile,*
>
> *Neighing in likeness of a filly foal.*
>
> *(II.i.)*

In Act II, Puck says these words in response to an unnamed fairy who identifies Puck and celebrates his infamous mischief. Here Puck describes the role he plays for Oberon, which is not unlike that of a jester, albeit a magical one. In the particular example he gives here, Puck amuses Oberon by tricking a horse into thinking he's a young mare.

> *Then fate o'errules that, one man holding troth,*
>
> *A million fail, confounding oath on oath.*
>
> *(III.ii.)*

Puck says this line in Act III, responding to Oberon's frustration that Puck applied the charm to the wrong person; he was meant to charm Demetrius, but charmed Lysander by mistake. With these words Puck implies that fault must not ultimately lie with him, but with fate. Puck declares that for each man who keeps his word, as he himself has done, a million others do not.

> *And those things do best please me*
>
> *That befall preposterously.*
>
> *(III.ii.)*

In Act III Puck utters these words to express his love of mischief. His use of the word "preposterously" is significant. The word derives from the Latin prepositions *prae* (in front of, before) and *posterus* (behind, after). Thus the word literally means "back first." In the Renaissance period "preposterous" was used to describe inversions of the normal order of things, and especially of social and sexual norms. It therefore suggested monstrosity and perversity. Puck clearly enjoys the perversity of such inversions.

> *If we shadows have offended,*
>
> *Think but this, and all is mended—*
>
> *That you have but slumbered here*
>
> *While these visions did appear.*
>
> *And this weak and idle theme,*
>
> *No more yielding but a dream,*
>
> *Gentles, do not reprehend.*
>
> *(V.i.)*

STUDY GUIDE

These are Puck's parting words to the audience at the end of Act V. Here the word "shadows" refers to the actors in the play that now comes to a close. Puck's words echo a speech Oberon gave earlier in the play, when he said the lovers, upon waking, would consider their night in the forest but a harmless dream. Puck encourages us to think the same about the play. No one should leave feeling disturbed by what they've seen. In this sense, Puck's closing words also echo the concerns the craftsmen had about not offending their audience, lest they face dire consequences.

HELENA

> I am your spaniel. And, Demetrius,
>
> The more you beat me, I will fawn on you.
>
> Use me but as your spaniel—spurn me, strike me,
>
> Neglect me, lose me. Only give me leave,
>
> Unworthy as I am, to follow you.
>
> (II.i.)

In Act II, after telling Demetrius about Hermia and Lysander's plan to run away, Helena follows Demetrius into the forest. We can hear desperation in Helena's hyperbolic language here. If taken at her word, Helena appears to desire Demetrius so badly that she's willing to subjugate herself completely, even sacrifice her own well-being. However, Helena could also be deliberately overstating her feelings, using irony to indicate the absurd, dog-like situation she finds herself in.

> Run when you will, the story shall be changed.
>
> Apollo flies and Daphne holds the chase.
>
> The dove pursues the griffin. The mild hind
>
> Makes speed to catch the tiger—bootless speed,
>
> When cowardice pursues and valor flies.
>
> (II.i.)

While chasing after Demetrius in Act II, Helena observes that her situation reverses traditional stories of pursuit. Whereas in the stories Apollo chases Daphne, the griffin chases the dove, and the tiger chases the deer (i.e., "hind"), here the hunter has become the hunted. Helena goes so far as to call her situation "a scandal on [her] sex." According to her, women "should be wooed and were not made to woo."

> *When truth kills truth, O devilish holy fray!*
>
> *(III.ii.)*

In Act III Helena uses this dense, punning language to rebuke Lysander for having abandoned Hermia. The basic sense of Helena's play on words is that Lysander has used the "truth" of his current love for Helena to negate the "truth" of his former love for Hermia. He has therefore acted in ways both "devilish" and "holy"—devilish, because he's betrayed one vow, and holy, since he's pledged another one.

THESEUS

> *Now, fair Hippolyta, our nuptial hour*
>
> *Draws on apace. Four happy days bring in*
>
> *Another moon. But oh, methinks how slow*
>
> *This old moon wanes! She lingers my desires,*
>
> *Like to a stepdame or a dowager*
>
> *Long withering out a young man's revenue.*
>
> *(I.i.)*

These are the first lines of the play, and in them Theseus expresses impatience for the night of his wedding with Hippolyta. The metaphor Theseus uses here is a bit strange, since he compares his situation to an impatient son waiting for his inheritance. In this situation, the slowly waning moon is like an old widow who holds on to her husband's possessions, thereby spurning her son.

By comparing love to wealth, Theseus signals from the beginning that he does not possess an ideal understanding of love.

> *More strange than true. I never may believe*
>
> *These antique fables nor these fairy toys.*
>
> *Lovers and madmen have such seething brains,*
>
> *Such shaping fantasies, that apprehend*
>
> *More than cool reason ever comprehends.*
>
> *The lunatic, the lover, and the poet*
>
> *Are of imagination all compact.*
>
> *(V.i.)*

In Act V, after the four lovers have returned to Athens and relayed the story of their night in the forest, Theseus tells Hippolyta that he doesn't believe their story. Instead, he sees the lovers' tale as the product of a confused and deluded imagination, not unlike the imagination of "the lunatic" and "the poet." Theseus's refusal to believe the lovers once again signals his narrow-minded attitudes about love.

> *The kinder we, to give them thanks for nothing.*
>
> *Our sport shall be to take what they mistake.*
>
> *And what poor duty cannot do, noble respect*
>
> *Takes it in might, not merit.*
>
> *(V.i.)*

Theseus announces his intention in Act V to watch the crafts-men's performance with suspended judgment and a generosity of spirit. He suspects that the performance will not be stellar, but as he explains to Hippolyta, his noble status means he must employ a generous judgment that places more value on effort than achieve-ment (i.e., "in might, not merit"). Theseus's attitude here couldn't be more different from the harsh, patriarchal attitude he espoused at the beginning of the play, which may indicate a softening now that all previous tensions have settled.

HERMIA

So will I grow, so live, so die, my lord,

Ere I will my virgin patent up

Unto his lordship, whose unwishèd yoke

My soul consents not to give sovereignty.

(I.i.)

After Theseus commands Hermia to obey her father's wish for her to marry Demetrius instead of Lysander, Hermia utters these words of defiance. Specifically, she rejects the idea that men should have any influence over who she loves and how and when she decides to yield her "virgin patent up." By claiming "sovereignty" over her own soul, Hermia issues a powerful statement of female autonomy.

If then true lovers have been ever crossed,

It stands as an edict in destiny.

(I.i.)

Following the scene where Theseus issues an ultimatum and outlines Hermia's punishment if she persists in her disobedience, Hermia confesses to Lysander that fate must have doomed their love. Hermia's reference to fate and the possibility that she and Lysander are cosmically "crossed" echoes the language of *Romeo and Juliet*, the play Shakespeare wrote just before *Midsummer*. Of course, while the earlier play about "star-crossed lovers" ended tragically, this play ends happily.

And are you grown so high in his esteem

Because I am so dwarfish and so low?

How low am I, thou painted maypole? Speak.

(III.ii.)

Hermia directs these lines toward Helena in the midst of their intensifying quarrel in Act III. While Helena frequently complains that she is less beautiful than Hermia, here Hermia uses punning language to imply her frustration at being shorter than Helena. But Hermia's words are also barbed. When she calls Helena a "painted maypole," she comments on her height as well as her use of cosmetics, implying that any beauty Helena has comes from makeup. The cruelty evident in these words indicates that the friends have hit rock bottom, descending to the point of base name-calling.

> *Methinks I see these things with parted eye,*
>
> *When everything seems double.*
>
> *(IV.i.)*

In Act IV, after morning has arrived and the fairy charms have worn off, Hermia still feels the residue of the night's confusion. She likens this feeling to the experience of seeing double. With these words Hermia references the prominent theme of doubling threaded throughout the play, embodied by the doubling of the human and fairy realms as well as the double pair of lovers.

11

WHAT DOES THE ENDING MEAN?

AFTER THE CRAFTSMEN conclude their rendition of *Pyramus and Thisbe* and Theseus calls for all of the lovers to go to bed, the fairies offer a blessing for the three sleeping couples. Oberon utters this blessing himself, saying, "Never mole, harelip, nor scar / Nor mark prodigious, such as are / Despised in nativity / Shall upon their children be" (V.i.). Oberon's words aim to prevent deformities among any children the Athenian lovers might conceive. Most obviously, this anxiety about deformity echoes the amorous pairing between Titania and Nick Bottom that occurred earlier in the play. Aside from its absurdity, Titania and Bottom's coupling is also shocking for its suggestion of bestiality. With his head having been "translated" into that of a donkey, Bottom is no longer strictly human. Given the play's implication that Titania and Bottom sleep together, Shakespeare's contemporary audience would have believed this near-bestial union capable of producing some kind of hybrid monster, hideously deformed as a mark of their parents' sin. Oberon's attempt to ward off deformities also has deep relevance to the mythical backstory of the play, and particularly to stories involving Theseus. One of the most famous myths to feature Theseus is that of the Minotaur, a monster with a man's body and a bull's head. The Minotaur was the offspring of Pasiphaë, who mated with the bull most prized by her husband, King Minos of Crete. Horrified by the result of this coupling, Minos employed the architect Daedalus to build a labyrinth in which to imprison the Minotaur. Part of what made the Minotaur so monstrous is that he survived on human flesh, and required a continuous supply of human sacrifices. After defeating Athens in war, Minos demanded that every nine years seven Athenian boys and seven Athenian girls be sacrificed to the Minotaur. When the third round of sacrifices came around, Theseus volunteered to be sacrificed. After arriving in Crete and navigating to the center of the labyrinth, he decapitated the Minotaur. Oberon's blessing may therefore echo the efforts of Theseus, his counterpart in the human realm, to rid the world of monstrous deformities and keep the peace.

12

HOW TO WRITE
LITERARY ANALYSIS

WHEN YOU READ FOR PLEASURE, your only goal is enjoyment. You might find yourself reading to get caught up in an exciting story, to learn about an interesting time or place, or just to pass the time. Maybe you're looking for inspiration, guidance, or a reflection of your own life. There are as many different, valid ways of reading a book as there are books in the world.

When you read a work of literature in an English class, however, you're being asked to read in a special way: you're being asked to perform *literary analysis*. To analyze something means to break it down into smaller parts and then examine how those parts work, both individually and together. Literary analysis involves examining all the parts of a novel, play, short story, or poem—elements such as character, setting, tone, and imagery—and thinking about how the author uses those elements to create certain effects.

A LITERARY ESSAY IS NOT A BOOK REVIEW

You're not being asked whether or not you liked a book or whether you'd recommend it to another reader. A literary essay also isn't like the kind of book report you wrote when you were younger, where your teacher wanted you to summarize the book's action. A high school– or college-level literary essay asks, "How does this piece of literature actually work?" "How does it do what it does?" and, "Why might the author have made the choices he or she did?"

The Seven Steps

No one is born knowing how to analyze literature; it's a skill you learn and a process you can master. As you gain more practice with this kind of thinking and writing, you'll be able to craft a method that works best for you. But until then, here are seven basic steps to writing a well-constructed literary essay:

1. Ask questions

2. Collect evidence

3. Construct a thesis

4. Develop and organize arguments

5. Write the introduction

6. Write the body paragraphs

7. Write the conclusion

1. ASK QUESTIONS

When you're assigned a literary essay in class, your teacher will often provide you with a list of writing prompts. Lucky you! Now all you have to do is choose one. Do yourself a favor and pick a topic that interests you. You'll have a much better (not to mention easier) time if you start off with something you enjoy thinking about. If you are asked to come up with a topic by yourself, though, you might start to feel a little panicked. Maybe you have too many ideas—or none at all. Don't worry. Take a deep breath and start by asking yourself these questions:

> **What struck you?** Did a particular image, line, or scene linger in your mind for a long time? If it fascinated you, chances are you can draw on it to write a fascinating essay.

What confused you? Maybe you were surprised to see a character act in a certain way, or maybe you didn't understand why the book ended the way it did. Confusing moments in a work of literature are like a loose thread in a sweater: if you pull on it, you can unravel the entire thing. Ask yourself why the author chose to write about that character or scene the way he or she did and you might tap into some important insights about the work as a whole.

Did you notice any patterns? Is there a phrase that the main character uses constantly or an image that repeats throughout the book? If you can figure out how that pattern weaves through the work and what the significance of that pattern is, you've almost got your entire essay mapped out.

Did you notice any contradictions or ironies? Great works of literature are complex; great literary essays recognize and explain those complexities. Maybe the title totally disagrees with the book's subject matter. Maybe the main character acts one way around his family and a completely different way around his friends and associates. If you can find a way to explain a work's contradictory elements, you've got the seeds of a great essay.

At this point, you don't need to know exactly what you're going to say about your topic; you just need a place to begin your exploration. You can help direct your reading and brainstorming by formulating your topic as a *question*, which you'll then try to answer in your essay. The best questions invite critical debates and discussions, not just a rehashing of the summary. Remember, you're looking for something you can *prove* or *argue* based on evidence you find in the text. Finally, remember to keep the scope of your question in mind. Is this a topic you can adequately address within the word or page limit you've been given? Conversely, is this a topic big enough to fill the required length?

STUDY GUIDE

GOOD QUESTIONS

"Are Romeo and Juliet's parents responsible for the deaths of their children?"

"Why doesn't Hamlet kill Claudius right away?"

"Is Lady Macbeth a villain or a victim?"

BAD QUESTIONS

"What happens to Nick Bottom in A Midsummer Night's Dream?*"*

"What do the other characters in Julius Caesar *think about Caesar?"*

"How does Iago remind me of my brother?"

2. COLLECT EVIDENCE

Once you know what question you want to answer, it's time to scour the book for things that will help you answer it. Don't worry if you don't know what you want to say yet—right now you're just collecting ideas and material and letting it all percolate. Keep track of passages, symbols, images, or scenes that deal with your topic. Eventually, you'll start making connections between these examples, and your thesis will emerge.

Here's a brief summary of the various parts that compose each and every work of literature. These are the elements that you will analyze in your essay, and that you will offer as evidence to support your arguments.

ELEMENTS OF STORY

These are the *whats* of the work—what happens, where it happens, and to whom it happens.

Plot: All of the events and actions of the work.

Character: The people who act and are acted upon in a literary work. The main character of a work is known as the *protagonist*.

Conflict: The central tension in the work. In most cases, the protagonist wants something, while opposing forces (antagonists) hinder the protagonist's progress.

Setting: When and where the work takes place. Elements of setting include location, time period, time of day, weather, social atmosphere, and economic conditions.

Narrator: The person telling the story. The narrator may straightforwardly report what happens, convey the subjective opinions and perceptions of one or more characters, or provide commentary and opinion in his or her own voice.

Themes: The main idea or message of the work—usually an abstract idea about people, society, or life in general. A work may have many themes, which may be in conflict with one another.

ELEMENTS OF STYLE

These are the *hows*—how the characters speak, how the story is constructed, and how language is used throughout the work.

Structure and organization: *How the parts of the work are assembled.* Some novels are narrated in a linear, chronological fashion, while others skip around in time. Some plays follow a traditional three- or five-act structure, while others are a series of loosely connected scenes. Some authors deliberately leave gaps in their works, leaving readers to puzzle out the missing information. A work's structure and organization can tell you a lot about the kind of message it wants to convey.

Point of view: *The perspective from which a story is told.* In *first-person point of view*, the narrator involves himself- or herself in the story. ("I went to the store"; "We watched in horror as the bird slammed into the window.") A first-person narrator is usually the protagonist of the work, but not always. In *third-person point of view*, the narrator does not participate in the story. A third-person narrator may closely follow a specific character, recounting that individual character's thoughts or experiences, or it may be what we call an *omniscient* narrator. Omniscient narrators see and know all: they can witness any event in any time or place and are privy to the inner thoughts and feelings of all characters. Remember that the narrator and the author are not the same thing!

Diction: *Word choice.* Whether a character uses dry, clinical language or flowery prose with lots of exclamation points can tell you a lot about his or her attitude and personality.

Syntax: *Word order and sentence construction.* Syntax is a crucial part of establishing an author's narrative voice. Shakespeare, for example, is known for writing in iambic pentameter, intermingling prose and verse, and scrambling the usual word order of a sentence.

Tone: *The mood or feeling of the text.* Diction and syntax often contribute to the tone of a work. A novel written in short, clipped sentences that use small, simple words might feel brusque, cold, or matter-of-fact.

Imagery: *Language that appeals to the senses*; representing things that can be seen, smelled, heard, tasted, or touched.

Figurative language: *Language that is not meant to be interpreted literally.* The most common types of figurative language are *metaphors* and *similes*, which compare two unlike things in order to suggest a similarity between them —for example, *"All the world's a stage,"* or *"I'll warrant him, as gentle as a lamb."* (Metaphors say one thing is another thing; similes claim that one thing is *like* another thing.)

3. CONSTRUCT A THESIS

When you've examined all the evidence you've collected and know how you want to answer the question, it's time to write your thesis statement. A *thesis* is a claim about a work of literature that needs to be supported by evidence and arguments. The thesis statement is the heart of the literary essay, and the bulk of your essay will be spent trying to prove this claim. A good thesis will be:

Arguable. "*Julius Caesar* describes the political turmoil in Rome after the murder of Julius Caesar" isn't a thesis—it's a fact.

Provable through textual evidence. "*Hamlet* is a confusing but ultimately very well-written play" is a weak thesis because it offers the writer's personal opinion about the book. Yes, it's arguable, but it's not a claim that can be proved or supported with examples taken from the play itself.

Surprising. "Viola changes a great deal in *Twelfth Night*" is a weak thesis because it's obvious. A really strong thesis will argue for a reading of the text that is not immediately apparent.

Specific. "The relationships in *A Midsummer Night's Dream* tell us a lot about the fickle nature of romance" is almost a good thesis statement, but it's still too vague. What does the writer mean by "a lot"? How do the relationships tell us about the fickle nature of romance?

GOOD THESIS STATEMENTS

Question: In *Romeo and Juliet*, which is more powerful in shaping the lovers' story: fate or foolishness?

Thesis: "Though Shakespeare defines Romeo and Juliet as 'star-crossed lovers' and images of stars and planets appear throughout the play, a closer examination of that celestial imagery reveals that the stars are merely witnesses to the characters' foolish activities and not the causes themselves."

Question: Does Hamlet's misogyny prove his madness?

Thesis: "Hamlet's misogynistic behavior toward Gertrude and Ophelia can be seen as evidence that he really is going mad, because these scenes have little to do with his quest for justice, and yet they seem to provoke his strongest feelings. We see little evidence in the play that either Gertrude or Ophelia is guilty of any wrongdoing, yet he treats them both with paranoia and cruelty, suggesting that Hamlet has lost the ability to accurately interpret other people's motivations."

Question: How does blood function as a symbol in Macbeth?

Thesis: "Once Macbeth and Lady Macbeth embark on their murderous journey, blood comes to symbolize their guilt, and they begin to feel that their crimes have stained them in a way that cannot be washed clean. Blood becomes a permanent stain on the consciences of both characters, and it plagues them throughout life."

4. DEVELOP AND ORGANIZE ARGUMENTS

The reasons and examples that support your thesis will form the middle paragraphs of your essay. Since you can't really write your thesis statement until you know how you'll structure your argument, you'll probably end up working on steps 3 and 4 at the same time.

There's no single method of argumentation that will work in every context. One essay prompt might ask you to compare and contrast two characters, while another asks you to trace an image through a given work of literature. These questions require different kinds of answers and therefore different kinds of arguments. Below, we'll discuss three common kinds of essay prompts and some strategies for constructing a solid, well-argued case.

TYPES OF LITERARY ESSAYS

Compare and contrast

Compare and contrast the characters of King Lear and Gloucester in King Lear.

Chances are you've written this kind of essay before. In an academic literary context, you'll organize your arguments the same way you would in any other class. You can either go *subject by subject* or *point by point*. In the former, you'll discuss one character first and then the second. In the latter, you'll choose several traits (attitude toward life, social status, images and metaphors associated with the character) and devote a paragraph to each. You may want to use a mix of these two approaches—for example, you may want to spend a paragraph apiece broadly sketching King Lear's and Gloucester's personalities before transitioning into a paragraph or two describing a few key points of comparison. This can be a highly effective strategy if you want to make a counterintuitive argument—that, despite seeming to be totally different, the two objects being compared are actually similar in a very important way (or vice versa). Remember that your essay should reveal something fresh or unexpected about the text, so think beyond the obvious parallels and differences.

Trace

Choose an image—for example, birds, knives, or eyes—and trace that image throughout Macbeth.

Sounds pretty easy, right? All you need to do is read the play, underline every appearance of a knife in *Macbeth*, and then list them in your essay in the order they appear, right? Well, not exactly. Your teacher doesn't want a simple catalog of examples. He or she wants to see you make *connections* between those examples—that's the difference between summarizing and analyzing. In the *Macbeth* example above, think about the different contexts in which knives appear in the play and to what effect. In *Macbeth*, there are real knives and imagined knives; knives that kill and knives that simply threaten. Categorize and classify your examples to give them some order. Finally, always keep the overall effect in mind. After you choose and analyze your examples, you should come to some greater understanding about the work, as well as your chosen image, symbol, or phrase's role in developing the major themes and stylistic strategies of that work.

Debate

Does Iago in Othello *hate women?*

In this kind of essay, you're being asked to debate a moral, ethical, or aesthetic issue regarding the work. You might be asked to judge a character or group of characters (*Is Caesar responsible for his own demise?*) or the work itself (*Is* Romeo and Juliet *a feminist play?*). For this kind of essay, there are two important points to keep in mind. First, don't simply base your arguments on your personal feelings and reactions. Every literary essay expects you to read and analyze the work, so search for evidence in the text. What does Iago have to say about women in *Othello*? How does Iago treat women in *Othello*? As in any debate, you also need to make sure that you define all the necessary terms before you begin to argue your case.

What does it mean to hate a whole gender? What makes a play feminist? You should define your terms right up front, in the first paragraph after your introduction.

Second, remember that strong literary essays make contrary and surprising arguments. Try to think outside the box. In the *Othello* example above, it seems like the obvious answer would be yes, Iago hates women. But can you think of any arguments for the opposite side? Even if your final assertion is that the play depicts an angry, misogynistic man who distrusts women, acknowledging and responding to the counterargument will strengthen your overall case.

5. WRITE THE INTRODUCTION

Your introduction sets up the entire essay. It's where you present your topic and articulate the particular issues and questions you'll be addressing. It's also where you, as the writer, introduce yourself to your readers. A persuasive literary essay immediately establishes its writer as a knowledgeable, authoritative figure.

An introduction can vary in length depending on the overall length of the essay, but in a traditional five-paragraph essay it should be no longer than one paragraph. However long it is, your introduction needs to:

Provide any necessary context. Your introduction should situate the reader and let him or her know what to expect. What book are you discussing? Which characters? What topic will you be addressing?

Answer the "So what?" question. Why is this topic important, and why is your particular position on the topic noteworthy? Ideally, your introduction should pique the reader's interest by suggesting how your argument is surprising or otherwise counterintuitive. Literary essays make unexpected connections and reveal less-than-obvious truths.

Present your thesis. This usually happens at or very near the end of your introduction.

Indicate the shape of the essay to come. Your reader should finish reading your introduction with a good sense of the scope of your essay as well as the path you'll take toward proving your thesis. You don't need to spell out every step, but you do need to suggest the organizational pattern you'll be using.

Your introduction should not:

Be vague. Beware of the two killer words in literary analysis: *interesting* and *important*. Of course the work, question, or example is interesting and important—that's why you're writing about it!

Open with any grandiose assertions. Many student readers think that beginning their essays with a flamboyant statement such as "Since the dawn of time, writers have been fascinated with the topic of free will" makes them sound important and commanding. You know what? It actually sounds pretty amateurish.

Wildly praise the work. Another typical mistake student writers make is extolling the work or author. Your teacher doesn't need to be told that "Shakespeare is perhaps the greatest writer in the English language." You can mention a work's reputation in passing—by referring to *Romeo and Juliet* as "Shakespeare's enduring classic," for example—but don't make a point of bringing it up unless that reputation is key to your argument.

Go off-topic. Keep your introduction streamlined and to the point. Don't feel the need to throw in all kinds of bells and whistles in order to impress your reader—just get to the point as quickly as you can without skimping on any of the required steps.

STUDY GUIDE

6. WRITE THE BODY PARAGRAPHS

Once you've written your introduction, you'll take the arguments you developed in step 4 and turn them into your body paragraphs. The organization of this middle section of your essay will largely be determined by the argumentative strategy you use, but no matter how you arrange your thoughts, your body paragraphs need to do the following:

Begin with a strong topic sentence. Topic sentences are like signs on a highway: they tell the readers where they are and where they're going. A good topic sentence not only alerts readers to what issue will be discussed in the following paragraph but also gives them a sense of what argument will be made about that issue. "Jealousy plays an important role in *A Midsummer Night's Dream*" isn't a strong topic sentence because it doesn't tell us very much. "Jealousy plays out most obviously among the quartet of Athenian lovers, who find themselves in an increasingly tangled knot of misaligned desire" is a much stronger topic sentence—it not only tells us what the paragraph will discuss (jealousy) but how the paragraph will discuss the topic (by showing how jealousy creates a set of conditions that leads to the play's climactic action).

Fully and completely develop a single thought. Don't skip around in your paragraph or try to stuff in too much material. Body paragraphs are like bricks: each individual one needs to be strong and sturdy or else the entire structure will collapse. Make sure you have really proven your point before moving on to the next one.

Use transitions effectively. Good literary essay writers know that each paragraph must be clearly and strongly linked to the material around it. Think of each paragraph as a response to the one that precedes it. Use transition words and phrases such as *however, similarly, on the contrary, therefore,* and *furthermore* to indicate what kind of response you're making.

7.   WRITE THE CONCLUSION

Just as you used the introduction to ground your readers in the topic before providing your thesis, you'll use the conclusion to quickly summarize the specifics learned thus far and then hint at the broader implications of your topic. A good conclusion will:

Do more than simply restate the thesis. If your thesis argued that *The Merchant of Venice* can be read as a study of religious differences, don't simply end your essay by saying, "And that is why *The Merchant of Venice* can be read as a study of religious differences." If you've constructed your arguments well, this kind of statement will just be redundant.

Synthesize the arguments, not summarize them. Similarly, don't repeat the details of your body paragraphs in your conclusion. The readers have already read your essay, and chances are it's not so long that they've forgotten all your points by now.

Revisit the "So what?" question. In your introduction, you made a case for why your topic and position were important. You should close your essay with the same sort of gesture. What do your readers know now that they didn't know before? How will that knowledge help them better appreciate or understand the work overall?

Move from the specific to the general. Your essay has most likely treated a very specific element of the work— a single character, a small set of images, or a particular passage. In your conclusion, try to show how this narrow discussion has wider implications for the work overall. If your essay on *The Tempest* focused on the character of Prospero, for example, you might want to include a bit in your conclusion about how he fits into the play's larger message about power, humanity, or the pursuit of knowledge.

Stay relevant. Your conclusion should suggest new directions of thought, but it shouldn't be treated as an opportunity to pad your essay with all the extra, interesting ideas you came up with during your brainstorming sessions but couldn't fit into the essay proper. Don't attempt to stuff in unrelated queries or too many abstract thoughts.

Avoid making overblown closing statements. A conclusion should open up your highly specific, focused discussion, but it should do so without drawing a sweeping lesson about life or human nature. Making such observations may be part of the point of reading, but it's almost always a mistake in essays, where these observations tend to sound overly dramatic or simply silly.

A+ ESSAY CHECKLIST

Congratulations! If you've followed all the steps we've outlined above, you should have a solid literary essay to show for all your efforts. What if you've got your sights set on an A+? To write the kind of superlative essay that will be rewarded with a perfect grade, keep the following rubric in mind. These are the qualities that teachers expect to see in a truly A+ essay. How does yours stack up?

- Demonstrates a thorough understanding of the book
- Presents an original, compelling argument
- Thoughtfully analyzes the text's formal elements
- Uses appropriate and insightful examples
- Structures ideas in a logical and progressive order
- Demonstrates a mastery of sentence construction, transitions, grammar, spelling, and word choice

SUGGESTED ESSAY TOPICS

1. Though Bottom often steals the show in performance, Puck is usually considered the most important character in *A Midsummer Night'ws Dream*. Comparing Puck to Bottom, why might Puck be considered the protagonist? In what way does Puck's spirit dominate the mood of the play? In what ways does the comedy surrounding Puck differ from that surrounding Bottom?

2. Compare and contrast the Athenian lovers with the craftsmen. In what ways are the dispositions of the two groups different from each other? Are they the same in any way?

3. What role do Theseus and Hippolyta play in *A Midsummer Night's Dream*? What is the significance of the fact that they are absent from the play's main action?

4. It has been argued that the characters of the Athenian lovers are not particularly differentiated from one another—that Hermia is quite like Helena (even down to her name) and that Demetrius resembles Lysander. Do you think that this is the case, or do you think that the lovers emerge as individuals? If you believe that these characters are quite similar to one another, what do you think Shakespeare's intent was in making them so?

NOTES

A+ STUDENT ESSAY

Many people have categorized *A Midsummer Night's Dream* as a romantic comedy. How accurate is this assessment?

A Midsummer Night's Dream, one of Shakespeare's most beloved comedies, is generally thought of as a sparkling romantic farce. However, while the play is lovely and comic, it also has a strong trace of darkness and cruelty, a sinister underside that is inextricable from its amorous themes. *Midsummer* may end with a series of happy weddings, but along the way it clearly depicts how male-female relationships can involve a great amount of cruelty, with the potential to spread discord throughout society.

Nearly all the male characters threaten their female counterparts with violence at some point in the play. Theseus, for example, won Hippolyta not through seduction or courtship but by military conquest, having vanquished the Amazons, her tribe of woman warriors. He says to her in the opening scene, "I wooed thee with my sword, / And won thy love doing thee injuries," drawing an explicit connection between love and assault. Later in the same scene, Egeus publicly threatens to kill Hermia, his daughter, if she does not consent to marry Demetrius. Oberon, for his part, does not put Titania at risk of true physical danger, but he does brainwash her with a love-potion for the express purpose of humiliating and humbling her. Lysander may be the only male who does not consciously seek to harm his mate. But even so, Hermia cannot escape peril. Just after the bewitched Lysander abandons her, she wakes from a nightmare, trembling with fear as she describes how she dreamt she saw "a serpent [eat her] heart away" (II,ii). Though Lysander isn't in control of his own actions at this moment, Hermia's subconscious still registers his desertion as an act of violation.

The female characters in the play, particularly Helena and Hermia, end up internalizing much of this violent behavior. In the most vicious exchange in the play, Lysander bluntly tells the lovesick Helena that he does not love her and that he is "sick" when he looks at her. He warns her that he will "do [her] mischief" in the woods—a far more menacing promise when we realize that mischief had a much stronger connotation in the period, meaning something closer to "harm" or "evil" than "naughtiness." Helena, however, is undeterred. She accepts the aggression directed at her and turns it into an argument for her stamina, pleading with him to treat her like his "spaniel," since the more he "beat[s]" her, the more she will "fawn" on him. Eventually, the two young women fall victim to the hostility in the air and turn on one another. Their confrontation in Act III, scene ii is often played as a comic catfight, but that ignores the poignancy of Helena's speech, in which she pleads with her "sister" not to "rent [their] ancient love asunder" by conspiring with the men to shame her. Hermia, however, does not listen, and the two dissolve into a torrent of mutual abuse. Even at the end of the play, when the couples are paired off harmoniously, it is unclear whether the women's intimate friendship will ever be repaired.

Throughout the play, romantic strife is portrayed as a force that can spread, like a contagion. At one point, the whole earth becomes infected. When the sparring fairy monarchs, Titania and Oberon, confront each other in Act II, scene i, Titania describes a tumultuous world filled with sickly clouds and rotting vegetation. She insists that this chaos has sprung from her and Oberon's quarrel, and that they are the "parents" of the planet's current state of turmoil.

A Midsummer Night's Dream ends with several happy (if magically-induced) weddings, but even the joy of the closing celebration does not completely banish the play's threatening undercurrent. The nuptials are commemorated with a clownish performance, but significantly, the craftsmen's theme is a gruesome one: a romantic couple that meets a violent and tragic end. In addition, the blessings offered by Puck and Oberon seem to evoke more terror than good will. Oberon offers the more traditional blessing, wishing the couples fertility and lasting love. However, he also mentions "blots of nature," (IV, ii) such as harelips and other deformities, calling attention to the dangers that can befall vulnerable children even as he wards them away. Puck, for his part, spends most of his speech describing all the horrible things that lurk outside the wedding chamber door, such as hungry lions and ghosts from "gaping" (IV, ii) graves. In the end, we don't know if the newlyweds are inside experiencing the flush of matrimonial bliss or if the discord that has been bubbling up throughout the play has unsettled them. As Puck closes the door against the terrible creatures of the night, he shuts the audience out, as well. With the ultimate fate of our protagonists so ambiguous, *A Midsummer Night's Dream* cannot properly be called a romantic comedy.

GLOSSARY OF LITERARY TERMS

Antagonist
The entity that acts to frustrate the goals of the protagonist. The antagonist is usually another character but may also be a non-human force.

Antihero / Antiheroine
A protagonist who is not admirable or who challenges notions of what should be considered admirable.

Character
A person, animal, or any other thing with a personality that appears in a narrative.

Climax
The moment of greatest intensity in a text or the major turning point in the plot.

Conflict
The central struggle that moves the plot forward. The conflict can be the protagonist's struggle against fate, nature, society, or another person.

First-person point of view
A literary style in which the narrator tells the story from his or her own point of view and refers to himself or herself as "I." The narrator may be an active participant in the story or just an observer.

Hero / heroine
The principal character in a literary work or narrative.

Imagery
Language that brings to mind sense-impressions, representing things that can be seen, smelled, heard, tasted, or touched.

Motif
A recurring idea, structure, contrast, or device that develops or informs the major themes of a work of literature.

Narrative
A story.

Narrator
The person (sometimes a character) who tells a story; the voice assumed by the writer. The narrator and the author of the work of literature are not the same person.

Plot
The arrangement of the events in a story, including the sequence in which they are told, the relative emphasis they are given, and the causal connections between events.

Point of View
The perspective that a narrative takes toward the events it describes.

Protagonist
The main character around whom the story revolves.

Setting
The location of a narrative in time and space. Setting creates mood or atmosphere.

Subplot
A secondary plot that is of less importance to the overall story but that may serve as a point of contrast or comparison to the main plot.

Symbol
An object, character, figure, or color that is used to represent an abstract idea or concept. Unlike an emblem, a symbol may have different meanings in different contexts.

Syntax
The way the words in a piece of writing are put together to form lines, phrases, or clauses; the basic structure of a piece of writing.

Theme
A fundamental and universal idea explored in a literary work.

STUDY GUIDE

Tone

The author's attitude toward the subject or characters of a story or poem or toward the reader.

Voice

An author's individual way of using language to reflect his or her own personality and attitudes. An author communicates voice through tone, diction, and syntax.

A NOTE ON PLAGIARISM

Plagiarism—presenting someone else's work as your own—rears its ugly head in many forms. Many students know that copying text without citing it is unacceptable. But some don't realize that even if you're not quoting directly, but instead are paraphrasing or summarizing, it is plagiarism unless you cite the source.

HERE ARE THE MOST COMMON FORMS OF PLAGIARISM:

- Using an author's phrases, sentences, or paragraphs without citing the source

- Paraphrasing an author's ideas without citing the source

- Passing off another student's work as your own

HOW DO YOU STEER CLEAR OF PLAGIARISM?

- You should always acknowledge all words and ideas that aren't your own by using quotation marks around verbatim text or citations like footnotes and end-notes to note another writer's ideas.

- For more information on how to give credit when credit is due, ask your teacher for guidance or visit www.sparknotes.com.

NOTES

NOTES

NOTES